Once again, Barbara Rector leads equine assisted facilitators on a path of expanding awareness by sharing her own life experiences of tragedy interlaced with wonder. It's a great ride!

Pam Salem,
HorsesTeachingandHealing.com

PORTALS TO MULTIDIMENSIONALITY

BARBARA K. RECTOR

Copyright © 2022 by Barbara K. Rector

All rights reserved.

No part of this book may be reproduced in any form or by any electronic or mechanical means, including information storage and retrieval systems, without written permission from the author, except for the use of brief quotations in a book review.

ISBN: 9798378758685

Portals to Multidimensionality Is dedicated to my Mom, Kathleen Louise Spriggs Wager Rector. Several years after my Dad's death in 1979, Mom would marry her first boyfriend, Paul Dayton. She divorced him when I was in treatment. As I became her rental tenant in Morningstar's outdoor bedroom, Mom attended a Foothills Yacht Club gathering guest of a garden club friend and met George Jones (Brigadere General George Jones, Ret) as he stopped to help her fix the broken heel on her shoe. At dawn the next morning she awakened me to say if he doesn't call she might have to call him. No need. As I'm leaving for work at 8 am that morning a dozen long stem red roses were delivered with a card suggesting a late lunch.

For all those who have ever wondered "for what purpose am I here?"

INTRODUCTION

"**Know that the answers are within yourself, and that the experiences through which the individual has passed on earth and in the interims between the sojourns on earth have made for abilities within yourself to coordinate the individual activity as to FIND the greater response from within than from any other source.**" Edgar Cayce

My work with Barbara has spanned decades. Each time she has shared her stories, I have stood in wonder and been amazed at the un-

INTRODUCTION

derlying Presence that guides and supports her. We came to know each other through the 'way of the horse' when we met at Bazy Tankersley's HAT Ranch in Arizona. Our shared reverence of these magnificent creatures and recognition of the deeper gift of awareness they hold for us created an instant and deep friendship. I was at my wit's end trying to find someone to help me understand what I was experiencing with my first-ever horse, Ticket. I could not find the words to express, nor did I fully understand the magical, soulful connection I felt whenever I was with him. Something as simple as cleaning his stall while he was eating created a profound sense of peace I wasn't feeling anywhere else in my life. I would also receive spontaneous insights or gain sudden clarity on projects or problems that I had been struggling with. I needed desperately to find someone who knew and understood "the unspoken."

On the first night of our gathering for the weeklong workshop, I realized I had finally found my teacher, mentor, and my soon-to-be new friend. I am forever grateful for the time

INTRODUCTION

and stories she has shared with me. I learned she knows of the mysteries we all sense in the depths of our hearts. I sat in astonishment as she told her teaching stories and encounters from around the globe. Many times, exclaiming "Only You Barbara!" only to hear her say "Oh no. It's not just me. You too, in your own way, have the gift. We all do."

It's the gift of perceiving beyond the ordinary 5 senses. The gift that many encounter when they connect deeply with their horse, a pet, the beauty in nature, or a sacred relationship.

I hope you can see in Barbara's life experiences- even and especially as they were hard and trying- the working of a sacred Presence being revealed. It is revealed in the soulful connection of a magical ride with a horse, the touch and care of a friend helping to repair a broken body, and in the timeless experience of two kindred souls moving together as one. Deeply soaking into my awareness, her stories continue to amaze me, abundantly revealing the profound mysteries that can be

INTRODUCTION

found in the ordinary experiences of daily life.

Delana Lands
Director Peaceful Spirit Ranch
Georgetown, TX USA

MEMOIR

I was born in 1942, so the year 2022 brings me to eighty years in this earth school. What remains for me to accomplish before my departure for the off-planet journey awaiting me on the other side of this very thin three-dimensional veil? Horses continue to teach me that there is 'more to life than meets the eye.' Science is showing that through the medium of the heart and brain, the equine heart captures our own. In the presence of horses, the human parasympathetic nervous system slows down, offering the human access to realms of realities not ordinarily available.

Multi-generational photograph of the Rector women. (Left to Right) Sister Wager, known to me as Danna, me holding Kelly, and my mom, Kathleen Spriggs Wager Rector.

Horses offer me the opportunity to explore the gap between the ordinary five-senses reality that makes up our daily life of 'to-do' lists, errands, family, tasks and chores, and civic and citizen responsibilities. I have come to depend on the shifted state of consciousness that comes about as I pause in my barn chores and lean against Brown to breathe synchronously with his slowed respiration rate. Great love and appreciation flood my heart.

Frequently the portal to the other realms opens and I am gifted with an awareness of specific next steps, or insight into a solution for a troubling situation. The shimmering glimmers of the vast pinkness voice feel I experienced so long ago (May 1973) and not yet if ever forgotten, "You must go back, my child. You are not yet done. There is more expected of you."

These stories are meant for anyone young or old who has ever asked themselves, for what reason am I here? For what purpose was I born at this particular time and place? What significance do my experiences offer in determining my life's purpose? What am I meant to accomplish? How do I contribute to this jewel of a planet we call home in the vastness of the cosmos?

That deep longing for felt love, being love, knowing love—oneness, unity, completeness—

has at intermittent intervals pervaded my life since. Even now I seek to integrate fully and coherently express that memorable near-death experience (NDE). For my nearly forty-eight years of wellness work with horses and humans seeking to teach relationship connections of the heart, I have learned to share the magic of this shifted state of consciousness offering to others a renewed sense of life purpose. Even if horses are not part of your daily life experience, the memory of a 'felt sense of unconditional loving, nonjudgmental "other" that is your own Magnificent Self remains.

N.D.E.

NEAR-DEATH EXPERIENCE

In May of 1973 in the oval of the First Avenue race track in Tucson, Arizona, I was competing in an A-rated hunter-jumper show sponsored by the American Horse Show Association. I was thirty-one, and I was riding Sel Rabi (barn name "Robbi"), a Minnesota-bred registered Arabian gelding who was just turning five. He had been green and started to walk, trot, and canter when the kids and I discovered him in a south Brainerd, Minnesota, barn. At nine years he had become an awesome jumper—one felt he could jump the moon—while remaining bold in the field following the hounds in the high grasslands of Sonoita, Arizona.

Sell-Rabbi at Grass Ridge Farms, Sonoita, Arizona.

PORTALS TO MULTIDIMENSIONALITY

Our discipline was a three-day event and I had arisen before daylight to meet my friend and field hunting partner, Gigi Sweet, to go show out of our trailers for one day of the week-long Race Track Show. Our trailers pulled into the parking lot at about the same time and we lined up to help each other with tacking and warmups. We planned to use the fixed jumps constructed for the four-foot hunter class as schooling for a big three-day event later in the month at Grass Ridge Farms.

Our horses were fresh in the predawn morning warm-up and yes, Robbi and I were feeling cocky. We were fresh off our big February win at the Scottsdale All-Arab show as Reserve National Open Jumper Champions. The early portion of our being on course was going well, when suddenly, we approached a large, square four-foot oxer of secured railroad ties with dirt piled between the rails to make an arch of five feet. Clearing both sides, ordinarily, nothing for us, I knew I was wrong on the approach but it was too late to abort. There was no give in the fixed obstacle as Robbi's knees hit the top of the first railroad tie element, catapulting us both into a giant somersault.

As we curved over, still together, my body instinctively began to roll on its own (I had been a five-meter board diver on my high school swim team) I hit the ground and continued my roll to flatten out, cracking my Caliente jockey helmet and eventually collecting 23 stitches down the back of my head, where I am still superconscious of the scar in my thinning and baby fine hair.

Robbi continued his somersault, head over heels, landing on his back, flat on my stomach with a harsh *thunk*! I didn't feel his landing on me as I was not in my body. I had cracked all of my vertebrae, all of my ribs, and my pelvic girdle, and had re-dislocated a shoulder that I had, in my youth, dislocated in a diving accident.

Robbi lay on me immobile, all four feet in the air. Indeed, we were both immobile and neither of us was breathing. The showgrounds paramedics and emergency veterinarian dashed up and found no vital signs registering in either of us. I was aware that my friend Gigi was coaching the ring stewards on how to wrap halter lead lines around Robbi's legs to roll him off my stomach. As the ropes started around his legs, Robbi shuddered and rolled off me.

If you have ever watched a horse leap to his feet after rolling out his kinks in sand or soft dirt, you know that they stretch out one foreleg to take all its weight as they spring up to stand. Robbi pushed off for his stand-up by putting his hoof on my outstretched hand. My right hand below the wrist took the full brunt of his 900 pounds and collected nineteen broken bones. I did feel that pain and popped back into my body.

I opened my eyes and felt Gigi's tears fall on my face. I said to her quite clearly, "I don't think my body works. Could you please take my contact lenses out?" We both wore thin plastic contacts that easily popped out as you pulled at the side of our eyelid. I felt Gigi remove each one; she placed them in the pocket of her rat-catcher hunt shirt.

Then the paramedics started fussing with me, wanting to gently roll me onto a flat board.

They had already placed a neck collar on me. No, I wasn't going to lay on any board to be carried in public. Unbelievably, I grabbed Gigi's wrist and asked her to help me up. She responded with firm full arm support and up I popped. Standing to brush myself off, I alarmed the medics, who had brought their truck up and wanted to help me get in the back for the trip to the University of Arizona emergency room.

"No," I said. "I will ride in the front passenger seat. But first, we are going around to the parked trailers to see and help Gigi load the horses." The vet had checked Robbi out and he appeared to be completely fine, registering all vitals in the normal range. The fact that I was upright and walking proved later to be all shock, adrenalin, strong personal will, and the need for control. Once Gigi had the horses loaded, she told the lot manager she would return later for my trailer and truck. She pocketed my keys and waved us off for the hospital.

On the sidewalk outside the entrance to the emergency room, they made me lie flat on a wheeled bed and the pain hit something stupendous. They administered no pain medication as there was uncertainty as to the extent of my internal injuries and whether surgery might be required. I hope to never live through another such x-ray exam; the required shifts in movement and positioning were excruciating. Eventually, I was packed in ice and sandbags and given a shot to keep my spinal cord from swelling and seeping into my fractures. Paralysis was a deep and real fear. My body locked down but my mind was working. I could talk and plead for pain relief, which gradually occurred as the ice took over its job of reducing the swelling.

Time passed as I was settled into a room, my right arm suspended in traction, my damaged hand swathed in gauze. The notion was for me to be immobile while my internal injuries were monitored and assessed. Husband Bob, whom I called Ram, entered the room with both kids. Kelly, five years, and Bobby, seven, both perched on the sandbags cradling me in bed. Kelly peered into my face and told me my eye makeup was on upside down! Bobby softly mentioned he once again spent most of his first-grade day in the corner, his teacher furious at his acting out behavior. Ram leaned over them both to kiss me and to include me in a family cuddle hug.

"Not to worry about being in the corner," I tell Bobby. "You are smarter than the teacher and she doesn't know how to keep you engaged and not so bored. We're going to fix that with an evaluation by a child psychiatrist specialist in education. It's clear to me as I visited you in your classroom today and was told what to do as an intervention by the Council of Lighted Beings."

Before an aghast Ram can say anything, I turn to Kelly and say, "Thank God you took Charlie to your Montessori classroom this morning. He's so much happier in a place with lots of people to admire him." I was sick and tired of Bobby's boa constrictor being loose in the house and scaring me witless as he dropped on my head through the laundry chute.

Now Ram is looking alarmed. "Honey, that man back east with whom you are doing that land deal is a full-out shyster; he's not being one bit truthful with you on the phone. I could hear both sides of your conversation this morning. Don't do the deal. Pull back and go with the other man who is honest and steady. The Council of Lighted Beings assured me that all would work out in the end."

The doctor comes in and Ram tells him that I appear to be hallucinating about some Council of Lighted Beings. Without missing a beat, the doctor asks if anything I am saying seems to make sense.

"Yes," responds Ram. "She appears to have been with us all this morning throughout our day."

The doctor tells him it appears that I and the horse have had a 'documented near-death experience'—a phenomenon that medicine is only slowly beginning to examine.

YES, I am churning inside with the recognition that I have somehow time traveled to Heaven, had an encounter with GOD, the shimmering Voice Feel Pink Light and a session with a Council of Lighted Beings that didn't go very well from my perspective. For days, I lay in fear of my body not ever working again. Occasionally, I caught glimmers of the warm pink flooding LOVE.

Before I left the hospital, nearly seven weeks later, I had mastered a practice of reverie retrieving felt/sense memory feelings of the Shimmering Pink Voice Feel of 'Now is not your time, my child.' The immensity of the surrounding LOVE cloud remains today a longing and a certainty for return when it is my time. First, my life purpose for being here in earth school at this time must be fully realized and complete.

Certainty of full restoration to function came well before the actual reality of my right side matching my left side with walking. That process would take two years. Five days after my incident, I knew from the Council it had not been an accident—that there are no accidents. Five days into lying immobile in the sandbags, my new friend Nancy McGibbon came to visit. I was astonished. She offered to pray with me, as we were such new friends we knew little to nothing about each other. We did have this ease of camaraderie, a shared enchantment by and love of the Arabian horse, and a capacity to talk endlessly about our kids who were quite close in age. Today, Feb. 2018, we remain the extended heart family of choice.

Nancy's prayer offered hope, compassion, and the joint feeling of accepting what was to be something we would deal with together. We didn't know at that time if my body and I would ever move around again. We would work to accept what is. Nancy did request that, if it were possible, my life in some manner be able to include horses. She was a physical therapist and had experience and knowledge of the awesome resilience of the human spirit in rehabilitation.

Once I was home with my family, my mom sent over her two maids to help with the housework, cooking, and care of the kids, leaving me free to do my physical therapy exercises and learn to navigate the several stories of our home in the foothills. The first week was rest and re-entry and visits to the barn, where our horses were stabled. Ram had shipped Robbi off to Chicago to a famed jumper trainer. I regret never having been able to see him again and say goodbye. (Robbi went on to set an indoor high jump record with a two-hundred-pound man on his back. His wall jump at six foot eight held the record for several decades.)

Nancy visited our barn and evaluated the situation, wondering if Ram's field hunter Bintina would be suitable for a desert walkabout. We both figured that for me to be astride a horse again would contribute greatly to mending the internal trauma of my feelings, thoughts, and emotions and easing my rehabilitation ordeal. Bintina was a caramel chestnut mare with a flaxen mane and tail—a registered half Arabian half Haflinger pony sized 14.1 hands. She was stout, with a solid temperament of sense and sensibility – abundant common horse sense.

Nancy agreed to help me get started, with the caveat that I manage the stall retrieval and haltering of Bintina, as well as the grooming, tacking, and putting away chores on my own.

Dwayne, the barn manager, built me a ramp mounting area attached to the porch of the concrete slab tack room building. We decided on a bareback pad, secured with the mare's hunt breast collar, side reins for her headstall with the rubber snaffle reins tied up around her neck. I was still wearing my half-body cast with right arm support. Nancy secured a neck collar that fit with my new hard hat.

I didn't ride Bintina. I sat astride her and when I was balanced and centered she agreed to walk off down the barn's various desert trails. It was like my early days with the burros riding us to school in Douglas. Nothing but the bamboo wands and the mutual agreement to take me and my siblings to school describes the fashion in which the two of us navigated our desert walks. Later, in my account, I return to clarify the reference to childhood burros.

In the beginning, Bintina chose to walk about the barn's desert foothills landscape for about twenty minutes. We did this routine daily, knowing that Dwayne would ride his gator out to find us should we stay out any longer than two hours.

After several weeks of home re-entry, I returned three days a week to the hospital for gait training classes. I was wearing a half-body cast that had a rod sticking out at an angle to hold my right arm elevated. My hand was left open, with a small ball to hold and squeeze. At the hospital, as I practiced with the other group members, all in their teens and early twenties, the doctor was baffled by my rapid improvement in balance and strength.

In about the second month of this routine, the doctor said to me something like, I don't understand it. You are a thirty-year-old woman and yet your recovery process is outpacing these youth in their prime. Your symmetry of gait is remarkable. I told him, "I ride every day."

His response was, "That's great. Writing in your journal is very therapeutic."

"No, not writing, though I do that too, with my dreams. I ride my husband's field hunter out into the desert every day."

The young doctor just stared at me, appalled. I was still in the body cast and rod. It would be another week or two before it was removed. "I wear a neck collar and a hard hat," I told him helpfully. His face was suffused with emotion and tears welled up. "If it's working so well for you, why don't you share it?"

Ah-ha. Those were fighting words to this Tucson Junior League executive committee secretary. I knew just what was required. Home I went for the first of several daily phone calls to Nancy. She lived on Santa Rita Ranch, high in the mountains south of Tucson. I lived in the northern Catalina foothills, across the vast desert basin from Mount Wrightstown, home of the McGibbon ranch. At the time, these phone calls were long-distance. They became so frequent and so expensive that the husbands bought us CB radios with which to communicate.

Here we were, two friends united in purpose, both believing in the efficacy of working with horses to build core strength and balance while exercising unused muscles. In the Divine way of the Universe, we were gifted with meeting Bazy Tankersley, who would become our teacher-mentor friend. Bazy was a new permanent resident of Tucson, having moved her Arabian breeding operation—(Al-Marah Arabians)—from Maryland to the Tanque Verde area. Al-Marah in Tucson was now located on three hundred acres off North Bear Canyon, quite near my own developing home on Wendell Road, within spitting distance of Morningstar (our family home as young adults with children).

BAZY

Bazy let it be known to the small tight Tucson horsey community that she intended to form an Arabian Horse Club to offer recognized Arabian horse shows as well as other club activities for non-competing members. Nancy called to suggest we attend the evening organizing meeting on Campbell Ave in a two-story bank building. I did not yet drive, so Nancy collected me, my walker, and a gait training belt for safety spotting when out and about in crowds. I wasn't comfortable in the bank's crowded elevator. By then, I was in a semi-half cast with my arm in a sling. I was fearful of being bumped; as any little thing could set off waves of pain. I would later spend several months wearing a TENS (Trans electric neural simulator) unit that gave me a mild shock if my body slouched into a pain-producing posture.

"We'll go up the steps," Nancy declared. She had done her homework and the fire escape exit door in the parking lot was open and ready for us. As we moved slowly up the dimly lit stairs, me leading and Nancy having my back, we approached an older woman in scuffed boots, frontier pants, and a pressed cowgirl shirt. She was carrying a worn leather satchel. The light over the door allowed me to look directly into her eyes. We locked onto each other, in silence, and then declared simultaneously: "I know you!" Nancy later said this raised goose bumps all over her neck, arms, and spine. She believed as we did that we knew each other. Yet, none of us had met (in this current lifetime).

We had met Bazy Tankersley.

After the meeting, which resulted in the formation of the Southern Arabian Horse Club, the three of us made our way down the exit door stairs to the parking lot. Bazy had heard a brief account of my incident and the doctor's challenge to us to help others experience the health benefits of horses and mounted work to build balance and strength. "We must do lunch. There is a woman from the United Kingdom at my farm in Maryland who teaches children and adults with hearing loss to ride. She is an instructor with Happy Horses for the Handicapped and is affiliated with Riding for the Disabled International."

Bazy gave us the phone number for her ranch office, with instructions to call and speak with Helen, her secretary, and get on her appointment calendar for lunch. Recognizing that we had found our key to how to get started, Nancy and I became determined to learn all we could about these other groups offering horses to people with disabilities, mostly located up and down the East Coast.

At our first luncheon meeting at a local Tanque Verde restaurant, Nancy and I watched from the porch as a bright yellow coupe with half a dozen various-sized dogs hanging out the open windows drove into the parking lot, Bazy at the wheel carefully seeking the largest patch of shade. Again, she was wearing scuffed boots, frontier pants, and a pressed cowgirl shirt, which we would learn was her signature garb. Carrying no purse, she strode up the steps to greet us. I muttered to Nance, "We're going to buy lunch."

During our meeting, which lasted close to four hours, an internal clock seemed to remind Bazy at regular intervals to go move her car to more shade and carry out more water for the dogs, who drank it from a large bowl on the floor behind the driver's seat. It was impressive, her instinctual animalness, or what I have come to seek in my students—their innate horsiness.

Bazy offered to invite her friend Maudie Hunter Warful to stay in her Tucson home for the summer and fall to help us get started on our program offering children and people with physical and cognitive challenges the experience of riding horses. There was a lot to do. We had to screen, select, and train suitable horses.

We needed to educate volunteers about our mission and vision as well as other organizations, such as the Arizona State School for the Deaf and Blind and the very receptive Flowing Wells School District. We also had to let them know about our readiness to provide services. We had to form a nonprofit organization and organize a board of directors.

The husbands, Bob Morken and Bill McGibbon were enlisted as truck and trailer drivers, side walkers, ramp builders, chief grooms, and babysitter lookouts for our kids, who served as model clients and patients. Our local east side pony club chapter operated out of our Wendell Road home barn and stalls, which contained several very suitable ponies and horses. Bintina was the star among them. Bazy offered her main Al-Marah arena, which was tree-lined and well-shaded, to be used on Sunday afternoons for practice sessions and volunteer training.

Bazy also offered several suitable Al-Marah lesson horses used for the internationally known Al-Marah apprentice program, credentialed through the U.S. Department of Education as a two-year post-high school graduate program. A person could earn an associate degree in animal science in that post-high school program, combined with classes in animal science at Pima Junior College and completion of the two-year work-study apprentice program at Al-Marah.

First two weeks of TROT property. The subsequent trees that outline the property

were planted by a Boy Scout looking to earn his Eagle Scout status.

In May of 1974, the husbands and the newly formed board of directors for TROT (Therapeutic Riding of Tucson, Inc.) raised the question of liability insurance. As I now lived almost next door to Bazy on Wendell Road, Nancy suggested I go over to the farm to ask her about insurance. We were still communicating primarily through our CB radios. We had learned by now that Bazy kept an open-door, open-office policy and that during morning and afternoon hours she could be counted on to be behind her desk.

While her main office building was under construction, Bazy's temporary farm office was in a single-wide trailer parked on an island near the creek. Dave Trexler, the Al-Marah farm manager, waved me through to the end of the hall and Bazy's open door. I knocked on the door frame and waited for her upraised head and greeting and invitation for me to come in and sit.

I got straight to the point. "It's about liability insurance for **TROT** and all our training here at the farm. The husbands and some of the board are very concerned. What do you do for insurance?" Bazy grins and beams at me. "Oh I'm covered," she declares and here she raises her hands and arms high in the air—"with the Great Above."

"Aaah," I respond, "I somehow don't think that will satisfy the husbands." Inwardly, I am affirming that we are going to be friends for life.

Bazy continues, "We'll propose to the new Arabian Horse Club that their first registered horse show will be to benefit the newly formed TROT and purchase both its liability insurance and its directors' errors and omissions policy. Initially, we'll go through Lloyds of London; they will insure anything for a big enough premium." Bazy knew what she was talking about and the proposal to the club was passed with several additional benefits, such as an education booth and, during the intermission, a brief demonstration by our early TROT riders and volunteers.

By August 1974 our little organization was humming along. Nancy and I would go to monthly meetings of Tucson Orthopedic physicians' education nights where you talk with professionals in the field and discuss a problem you might have with a patient and how you might proceed with it. We wanted them to know our service was available and what it might offer.

CHEFF CENTER STUDY

My daughter Kelly and I went to Michigan for six weeks in the early summer of 1975 to learn the principles and process of therapeutic riding from the Cheff Center's Lida McGowan. By the following year, Lida implemented her curriculum design used with myself and her daughter Bliss into what became NARHA's (North American Riding for Handicapped) first approved Therapeutic Riding Instructor course. Our daughters, both the same age and "D" pony clubbers larked about on the center's ponies, riding through the woods and even participating in cubbing with the Kellogg Hunt

Club. Cubbing is the practice of teaching the young hounds to pack up while hunting and always listening to the Master's horn.

Lida was an enlightened horsewoman who recognized her center ponies benefitted greatly from the daily cross-country workouts with the young competent girls. The girls gained experience riding a variety of ponies and small horses. Our six-week residential stay with Lida and Bliss at Cheff Center was possible as Ram was one state away in Minnesota at our summer Gull Lake home teaching Bobby to sail with the help of his parents. They made two lake crossings to visit us and experience our new friends at Chef. For the men in my family, it was all about the trip on the steamer with the car.

Husband Ram came home one hot afternoon and slapped down on the breakfast room table the annual issue of Forbes Magazine featuring wealthy individuals.

"No wonder she was rather casual with the insurance," he said, emphatically.

I looked down and there on the cover was

Bazy's picture and a headline about The Richest U.S. Women and How They Use Their Wealth. Also included was another Tucson woman, Tori Congdon, who was in our Junior League. Who knew? We had no idea they were wealthy, much less *that* wealthy.

After I read the long article listing Bazy as number one, along with pages about her background, her accomplishments, her achievements, and her status as the world's largest individual breeder of Arabian horses, I got on the CB radio to talk to Nancy. Bazy was also a significant owner of the Chicago Cubs! We both agreed, that we had no idea—none at all! At our first get-to-know-you lunch (yellow dog-filled car) we interviewed her to determine if we could count on her to do what she said she would do. **Whew!**

I promised Nancy that I would visit Bazy the next day, to make sure this new public knowledge would not affect our use of the Al-Marah arena and horses on Sunday afternoons. The next morning after doing my home barn chores, I again entered Bazy's office trailer, and Dave waved me back. Bazy was watching the door expectantly. "Aha!" She rose and came around her desk as I entered. "I know that neither of you knew. It wasn't important between us and the work we are called to do together. We will speak no more about it." She punctuated her words with a hug.

Bazy was not a demonstrative person so, for me, her volunteered hug served as a horse person's handshake: 'We have an agreement.' Bazy's only public reference to Nancy and me, and our work together came in a beautiful and interesting book about her called ...*And Ride Away Singing* published by Arabian Horse Owners Foundation.

In the summer of 1976 or 77, Bazy wanted me to ride some of her stallions in local horse shows. She would pay me to do so. Ram was hugely upset and wouldn't hear of it, feeling that "no wife of mine works." Okay, would it be acceptable for her to send me to a school for riding instructors at a small girls' school in Virginia? Yes, that was acceptable. Bazy wanted me to help introduce her apprentices to equitation, the art of riding horses—so they could learn about it while I was learning how to help Bazy's Al-Marah clients build a relationship with their newly purchased animals.

The Instructor School was accredited by the American Association of Riding Instructors. You could choose from different specialty disciplines for your focus, skills development, and testing for graduation. I chose cross country and hunter/jumper. As I was still one of the Tucson Pony Club instructors, I pointed out to Ram that in addition to teaching our TROT sessions and the developing instructors, I would get valuable continuing education experience from the Virginia school. And so it was decided and off I went to Virginia while Ram and the kids journeyed to our family cabin on Gull Lake in Minnesota and spent time with their paternal grandparents.

The late seventies and the eighties were full and busy. In 1978, my dad, Bill Rector, encouraged me to write a letter to his firm, Cooper Industries, to request tuition money for Nancy and me to travel to the United Kingdom to attend the World Congress on Riding for the Disabled International (RDI) to be held in Warwick, England. I gave them the facts about Therapeutic Riding of Tucson, Inc., and emphasized that the educational opportunity would give both of us more resources for developing services in our community. Cooper Industries awarded TROT a grant large enough to cover our travel expenses and tuition. Off we two best friends ventured. We could write a separate book about our adventures on that trip to the University of Warwick.

Bazy heard of our trip and told me that her ranch manager, Dave Trexler, was going to give a cutting exhibition at the Congress riding one of the Queen's imported Al-Marah stallions. Dave has his own remarkable story, a portion of which is featured in. Rama's Magic. (See reference -)

While he was serving in Vietnam, Dave's plane landed on a land mine in DaNang, which sent him rolling across the tarmac as a human fireball. The fire burned much of his handsome face, so he was tremendously shy about his appearance. After rehabilitation at the Denver VA Hospital, under the guidance of social worker Mary Woolverton, he began working with horses. Mary introduced him to her Morgan mare Hersey and he stopped believing that his life was over because he had lost both his legs.

Dave had become the farm manager at Al-Marah and had taken up learning to ride cutting horses—horses that, in partnership with their rider, demonstrate skill in separating (cutting) a single cow from a herd—sometimes from deep in the herd, and sometimes from the edge of it. At this congress, he would be riding one of the Queens' Arabian stallions, which carried a heavy Al-Marah Crabbet Stud pedigree. The pair would be filmed for television.

Dave is an awesomely talented man with a wry sense of humor who operates with sheer guts. From the very beginning, he offered TROT many specific suggestions and considerations about working with people who had severe challenges and who had also served in the military. Dave's refrain: "We are all people first." By now, he was active in North American Riding for the Handicapped (NARHA), which later morphed into the Professional Association of Therapeutic Horsemanship International (PATH Intl.).

RDI

RIDING FOR THE DISABLED INTERNATIONAL

Bazy asked Nancy and me to keep an eye out for Dave and his wife, Shirley, and to make him part of our group. On the walls of TROT, we have a great picture of Dave and his wife, Nancy and me, and the renowned Mary Woolverton meeting Princess Anne, the royal patron of RDI. There are some legendary stories about this trip that I tell later. After the Congress, Nancy arranged for the two of us to visit Grand Dame Edith, who lived in a castle. Dame Edith ran a local RDI program in a field beneath her family castle's moat—yes, a real moat. Our purpose was to learn more about adaptive equipment, volunteer training, and the process of creative thinking that goes into helping challenged youth and adults enjoy the benefits of horseback riding.

Our overnight and the entire next day in the field with Dame Edith and her RDI crew, as well as a formal "we dress for dinner on Fridays" second night, was an exhilarating and unforgettable experience. There were no electric lights on the second floor of the castle. We were given candles and the company of our footman who would take us down the hall to the loo upon request, which we signaled by ringing a bell next to our bed.

RDI Conference Warwick, United Kingdom. Princess Anne is in the foreground with Dave Trexler, me behind him, and Nancy McGibbon to Dave's right.

Back stateside, the two of us entered a frenzy of implementing the ideas and skills we acquired from Congress. We had outgrown our stay at Al-Marah's main arena on Sundays. We were operating programs three days a week and were now ready to implement a full day of what would later become known as Hippotherapy. Bazy decided she would fund a small stipend for a development director for TROT. Said job, she told her board, should also include the location of a new permanent home for TROT. Bazy suggested I was the obvious person for the job as I was currently also teaching the other instructors, training the new therapy horses we had acquired (we now had a roster of eight), and also teaching many of the more difficult classes.

Although Ram had initially been unwilling to allow me to work for pay, by now he felt differently as he experienced how often he cooked dinner and helped our kids with their homework as I was tied up essentially running TROT with Nancy's help. Nancy also functioned as our clinical director who offered physical therapy services and consults to those students requiring her specialty expertise. Ram decided my stipend would go towards a full-time housekeeper.

Wednesdays were sacred hunt days for me, Kelly, and Gigi. Gigi was one of the first therapeutic riding instructors we recruited; she also taught the local 4-H riding group. Kelly had permission from her second and third-grade teachers to miss school and hunt her pony, Dolly, with Gigi and me. Kelly handed in essays about her adventures with the Grass Ridge Hounds in the high grass country of Sonoita, AZ.

Saturdays, we rode our horses from the Wendell Road property through the Tanque Verde washes and desert trails several miles to the training barn of our riding coach on Wrightstown Road. Both Kelly and I participated in Jonas Irbinska's famous Saturday morning group riding lesson, where we never knew what was going to be the challenge. Of course, we returned home and wanted Dad and Bob to join us in these magical cross-country wash rides, and frequently they would. Both the Morken men rode quite well, but they preferred desert Tote Gotes, small motorized vehicles that zipped about the desert and foothills.

I became the TROT development director and began the search for a property of our own.

By this time we had moved off the island at Al-Marah and over to the cow arena where our board erected a portable tin shed for tack and adaptive equipment. The farm designated one of its large creek paddocks as TROT pasture to house our expanding therapy herd. But at the same time, a sense of unease and unrest was building in me.

One day in 1979 I answered the phone and learned from Chicago's Port Authority that my dad had dropped dead at Chicago O'Hare airport. In his wallet, they had found directions to call me should anything happen to him. I was directed to please tell my mom in person and then to have our family lawyer contact them about retrieving my dad's body.

Whew! First I called Ram.

"Well, Honey, do as they suggest," he said. "I'll go get the kids at school and meet you over at your mom's."

On the drive to Mom's house, I stopped at the local Circle K to buy a pack of cigarettes.

I had given up smoking when we lived in Minneapolis and I was pregnant with Kelly.

Having learned that I was expecting, Dad had sent his Lear to Minneapolis to collect me for a few days' visit with him and Mom in Saginaw, Michigan, where they lived. After a short flight and a strong building need to pee—no way was I using the porta john curtained behind the co-pilot—I could see my dad on the tarmac holding a copy of the *Wall Street Journal*. The headline: a surgeon general's report that smoking crosses the placenta's blood-brain barrier and endangers the health of the fetus. Uh-oh, I thought. I wanted a smoke.

The year was 1967. I bundled up little Bobby and we descended the stairs to hug his grandpa. My dad got right to the point. "I know what you are here to tell us. Look at this conclusive evidence against smoking."...Ahaaaa. "I have a proposal," he said. "What have you always wanted? Your life's dream is what?"

"Dad," I sighed, "you know my dream is a ranch in Arizona where I can have horses, near enough to town so the kids have good schools."

Dad didn't miss a beat. "Well, here is my deal. You give up smoking here and now and as soon as we get home to your mom, I write you a check for the land in Arizona and the money to build a house. If you ever smoke again in my lifetime, you have to pay the money back double."

Now, unconscious of my actions,—my thoughts, and my behaviors I am on autopilot, an addict returning to her drug of choice. In dreadful deep grief, released from my bargain with Dad, I am smoking a cigarette on the front steps of MorningStar. Mom answers the door and knows immediately and begins to wail. Instantly Lilliana and Aurorita appear to comfort and hover over her, urging us to sit in the gallery while they bring hot tea. Once Ram arrives, he takes charge--calling Bill Tinney, our family lawyer whose daughter Robin was in our pony club, and calling my sister and brother. He has me talk to them to repeat over and over the little information I have.

Mom had suffered from suicidal depression on and off all of my life. There were periods when she was truly good and functional, but there were also rather dreadful episodes. I now called Mom's psychiatrist to fill him in on the situation and affirm that he has room to see her in the morning.

Mom's depression emerged big time after she birthed me; the Holotropic Breathwork story confirms this. After the move to Michigan and Mom's serious suicide attempt, my sister Susan researched shock therapy being recommended by the treatment center; Mom consented. It appeared to give her extended periods of normality and required constant psychiatric supervision of her bloodwork and medication. Weekly psychoanalytic therapy first Freudian and then, Jungian contributed to stability.

This was the beginning of a major stress time for me. Chicago details that emerged required my immediate attention and action; my brother and sister both arrived with their families. Luckily MorningStar had a lot of bedrooms. After Dad's massive memorial service, when the nearly hundred out-of-town guests had departed, Mom suggested that I might need to see a counselor.

My dad had moved Mom to Tucson when it

became clear Tucson was the destination for me and my family. Dad's business in hardware manufacturing had grown and morphed into a conglomerate now known as Cooper Industries. Cooper's corporate offices were in Houston, Texas, and Dad's Lufkin Rule division (which manufactured tapes, rules, and other tools to measure things) was by then in Raleigh, North Carolina. He believed it was time to return to Tucson, where he and Mom had met.

I felt designated to be Mom's caregiver when Dad was not about. Without Dad in the physical (More about his Presence later.) Mom felt she could not live in MorningStar alone, so she leased a house in Tucson Country Club for her and the girls. She kept the yard service, AC Brown caretaker for the dogs and Morningstar, and packed her essentials to move to the new house. I had to check on MorningStar and determine that AC, (my Dad's man's man) had everything under control. But I was smoking over a pack of cigarettes a day and beginning to realize that I did not have myself under control;

I was becoming an anxious, nonfunctional wreck.

My psychiatrist had offices in the same building as Mom's doctor, so we often visited together and then did lunch. This was 1979 and even less was known about mental illness, effective treatment, and the genetic components of depression than is known now. I was prescribed an early-stage antidepressant and three psychoanalytic sessions a week.

GRIEF

The environment of the sixties and seventies that helped shape my young adult married life encouraged drinking. As a corporate couple following in my family's footsteps, Ram and I entertained frequently, especially in our foothills home. Alcohol flowed at these functions. I generally drank white wine—watering it down with ice for larger, longer evenings. That too would eventually get out of control.

During our move to the nearly completed Wendell Road home—the twenty-acre horse farm of my dreams, I answered the phone one day. It was the FBI. My Dad's plane had been hijacked. The FBI speculated that there might be a connection between the hijackers and my Dad's business interests. He was one of several frequent commuters on an American Airlines flight known to keep a regular weekly schedule. With business offices in Houston and Raleigh, Dad made American Airlines his weekly transport to work in Houston and then on to Raleigh. Departing from Tucson on Monday, he would travel this route and then Thursday evening take a flight up the East Coast to Newark, catch the Chicago connection, and change again at O'Hare for a direct flight to Tucson. The time differences worked favorably so he would be home for a late supper with Mom.

In any event, they were notifying family members of the passengers before the hijacking of a commercial passenger jet hit the evening news. Would I please go tell my mom in person? YES, and they would keep me apprised of the situation. I was given a number to call for further updates. The plane was in the air and had been diverted to Bangor, Newfoundland.

I called Ram and collected the kids for the short drive over to Mom. Ram would meet me there, bringing pizza. We called Susan and Walt, who brought their families from Phoenix to join us. Ram told them to pack for the weekend as we didn't know when Dad would be able to get home. We adults were scared. The cousins ran riot in the gallery, having invaded Mom's 'secret closet' with games, dress-ups, and art supplies. Lilliana and Aurorita bustled around, apparently happy with the mass confusion and with plenty to keep them busy.

Mr. Macgrabi, manager of Tucson's American Airlines, called to tell us that the hijackers had chosen a plane with no international flight capabilities, even though their demands included clearance for a flight over Paris to drop leaflets about the Croatian cause for independence. In Bangor, the plan was to offload some of the passengers and the entire cargo and luggage and take on more fuel. With a lightened load it was believed the plane could go the distance. The pilots reported optimism. Hijackers said once in Paris, and leaflets were released they were mission complete.

It was the sort of plane with a rear-door stairway exit. On the icy tarmac of Bangor airport, one of the pre-flight tasks was de-icing. Dad told us later that the hijackers appeared to him to be as scared as the passengers. One of them attempted to separate a mother and her child. Dad grabbed the kid and tucked him under his overcoat as all the passengers were being hustled off the plane—except for several nuns who volunteered to remain as hostages, claiming they had always wanted to see Paris.

Dad's actions of grabbing the kid apparently angered one of the hijackers, who shoved him, the last one off, down the stairs. The kid, cradled against Dad's chest, was unhurt. Dad's head required stitches and his body carried harsh bruises and road rash for weeks. Mr. Macgrabi kept us filled in on the unfolding events. Not until late the next day did we learn that Dad was off the plane and his not-too-serious injuries were being treated.

Late in the afternoon of the second day, Mr. Macgrabi arranged for our family vehicle to collect Dad directly off the tarmac as he left an American Airlines flight from Chicago. Most of us were crammed into my big Chevy Suburban, with Ram at the wheel. This was before seat belts were a concern and we bundled Dad into the second seat filled with Mom and five grandchildren overflowing the rear cargo space. Josh would come along after Dad's death followed by the winter I was in treatment. We drove around to the private plane lounge for stand-up hugs, restroom breaks, and a snack to hold us until home, where we would eat Lilliana's beloved Pozole.

Me in treatment? Dad left his body in early January 1979. I spent nearly the next two years trying to escape my grief. Ram agreed to breed my cross-country Trekhner mare, Natasha, to a highly reputed Trekhner stallion in Solvang, California. Natasha was aging out of the rigors of cross country and hunting and I took nearly a year researching potential sires—influenced by my work at Al-Marah, where I was learning breeding principles and genetics from Bazy and her vast private library.

When we were ready to go to Solvang, my friend and riding lesson buddy Jackie Severson, had a mare she wanted to send to a famed stallion also standing in Solvang. Jackie would pay us to haul Miss Meacham, her lovely Intermediare I personal horse. Ram was excited that the trip was moving into the paying-for-itself category. With two kids and two horses and the Suburban filled with must-take essentials, we had a flat tire chugging up a steep hill on the California freeway. Ram handled the situation superbly. We never needed to offload the horses. After delivering them to the stud farm and touring the place to see where Tash and Meacham would stay, we left to visit Gilroy, the garlic capital of the world.

My psychoanalytic sessions continued. What none of us knew and what medical science had yet to discover was the dangers of the interaction between the antidepressants, the valium for my anxiety, and the growing frequency of our party wine drinking. My stressed system was building up to full-blown alcoholism. Early Fall of 1981, fractures in my marriage were widening. My horse Tivo, Tash's baby, was found to be missing some essential brain cells. As he developed, his behavior was erratic and unpredictable, so we sent him to Jonas Irbinskas's training stables for evaluation and possible solutions. Vets deemed euthanasia the kindest option; more unacknowledged grief, buried in the business of life.

Ram refused to admit I was in trouble with my drinking, even though the kids told me he would come home and find me passed out in our bathroom.

My sister Susan intervened. "Barbara, you are killing yourself. You must get help."

By this time, Ram and I had agreed to a trial separation. Rather than him moving into a rental house, I chose to move there alone. Susan and her daughter Cynthia helped me move my essential belongings to a small rental home near Fort Lowell Park. The next day I awoke in my strange bed in my excrement.

That very morning I agreed for Susan to

take me to Phoenix and her doctor's psychiatric hospital for residential evaluation. During the check-in process at Scottsdale Camelback, my bags were examined and a list of my medications was charted. Susan urged me to sign myself into residential psychiatric care, so I could retain my own guardianship and avoid becoming a ward of the state. This was in November 1981. There was no Betty Ford Treatment Center yet; our first lady had yet to come out as an alcoholic. Society remained under the impression that women were not alcoholics, especially those who were highly functional with no public falling-down-drunk erratic behavior.

Ram is to be forgiven for his denial. His adopted Mom, Audrey, was so impaired by alcoholism that he, as a ten-year-old with rheumatic heart disease, had to be moved to his maternal grandmother's (May Carr's) for nursing and nurturing care. Ram simply didn't want an alcoholic wife. He refused to allow the kids to visit me in the hospital. Not until twenty-five years later was family week offered at Betty Ford as part of a residential professional week of education about the disease of alcoholism.

My treatment lasted a blessed three months. We patients called the campus of Scottsdale Psychiatric Hospital "Psy-U." Those of us who were residential came to love its cocooning safety and shelter from daily 'real world' issues. There were harsh moments, however. As my body slowly detoxed from the prescription drugs, without the softening effects of wine, my body began to scream in pain. I was given all sorts of alternative therapies, massage, ultrasound, physical therapy, psychodrama, art creative classes, and group and private psychotherapy sessions.

Little was known about drug dependence, trauma resolution, and alcohol abuse in 1981, so local experts lectured on family dynamics and effective treatments. Attendance at Alcoholics Anonymous meetings was considered the best and most effective approach, but at the time experts and members of AA disagreed about whether alcoholism was a disease. There were even questions about who should be identified as an alcoholic.

In hospital groups and later in visiting AA groups held at the hospital, I resisted declaring I was an alcoholic. The closest I came—and I celebrate 41 years abstinent in January 2023—is to introduce myself as "I am Barbara, a gratefully recovering alcoholic." After my wellness professional learning family group at Betty Ford, I now say most often, "Hi. I am Barbara, a gratefully recovering person with the disease of alcoholism."

Midway through my psychiatric hospital stay, my mom calls to say that Ram has informed her that I have used up my lifetime supply of treatment days under the family Blue Cross Blue Shield policy. Hmmm. The hospital director informs Mom and me that I am in no way ready to leave and require more treatment. I'm considered co-morbid with a mental health diagnosis of depression complicated with anxiety disorder as well as substance abuse.

PEPPER PIKE

Mom wants to know if I am willing to sell Pepper Pike, the young thoroughbred my dad purchased in California as my new competition horse, now that Tasha was retired. Mom has talked to Jonas and he believes he'll bring a good price from an LA jumper trainer. Pepper? Sell beloved Pepper Pike, a gift from my Dad? Mom questions how much value I put on my recovery. She can lend me the $35,000 plus cash to cover continuing hospital costs but is going to require restitution, which means selling Pepper. He is the only asset that is genuinely my own; a Prince Windy colt just four years old.

Tearfully, I agree. I call Jonas and plead that he promise to keep track of Pepper. If there is any way to have him back, I want the first right of refusal for his repurchase. Jonas agrees, as his wife Heather, who has been riding him while I was away, has made a similar plea. Pepper was a very special horse. And in the way of the Universe, Pepper would eventually cycle back into our lives.

First I have to complete treatment and achieve discharge, which includes two years of a regular weekly aftercare group and daily AA meetings. In the beginning, it is suggested that for the first ninety days out of treatment, I attend a meeting each day, sometimes more than one a day. In ninety days this daily practice trains you to become habituated to living life in sobriety and scheduling your days around a meeting.

On January 15, 1982, I am discharged from Scottsdale Camelback and advised to drive directly to a noon AA meeting in Tucson. I do just that. Scared beyond belief, I park my car in the Pima Alano Club parking lot on Pima Street, on the east side of Tucson, an area near my new home, the rental house near Fort Lowell Park. The large smoke-filled room of strangers is almost overwhelming but so is my desire to stay sober and follow my discharge plan. The tables are crowded; I sit between an older woman and a preppy man about my age. At the point when newcomers are invited to introduce themselves, I stay mute. My hands shake so much that I dare not light a cigarette.

I sit and listen in amazement. Whoever is speaking, what they say appears to contain portions of my story. As the meeting concludes, the moderator invites us to stand, hold hands, and say the Serenity Prayer. I say it reverently. With the final hand squeeze, both Jessie, the older woman, and Bill, the preppy man, turn to me and say, "New, huh?" and introduce themselves.

"Yes, I am new," I admit, "and very scared. Just out of the hospital in Phoenix. I don't know if I can find my car in the lot." Jessie pats my back and says, "Well, honey, we'll wait with you as the lot clears and your car will be easy to spot." They chat with me as we wait and Jessie offers me a cigarette. Bill opens the driver's door of my car and they both ask if I'm coming back to the 5:30 or the 8 p.m. meeting that night. I tell them, No, I'm enrolled in the O'Reilly Care Center aftercare program tonight." Bill waves goodbye and tells me he may see me there. Jessie gives me her phone number. She tells me she is my temporary sponsor and I'm to call her no matter what the time if I am sinking into feeling like I need a drink. She affirms the noon meeting is where to find her and she wants to see me there tomorrow.

I have been advised by the hospital not to return home until after the group session they have enrolled me in for that evening: Singles Aftercare at the O'Reilly Care Center. I drive to a grocery store for supplies, feeling strong and renewed. I have my first two sober friends. That evening at the O'Reilly Care Center it dawns on me that the hospital has assigned me to Singles Aftercare. There is no realistic hope of reconciliation with Ram, who doesn't believe I am a real alcoholic and maintaining my sobriety.

I agree with the intake counselor's request: I will give the first ten weeks an honest try. She affirms that I will learn a great deal about the family dynamics of the disease. So I accompany her to the singles group meeting room to be introduced to the moderator and the others. And who do you suppose is the moderator? Bill, the preppy man from the Alano Club noon meeting; is kind and generous with his smile. "Glad to see you made it." He explains to the others that we have met that day at the noon Alano Club meeting, but he leaves the story of my first out-of-treatment AA meeting for me to share. It is my story to tell. One group member remarks on the synchronicity of my day. She calls it a message from God.

Later at home alone, I affirm to myself that yes, the whole day has been like a message from God. My welcome-home phone conversation with Mom goes well and we agree I'll come to see her at her new country club rental after the noon meeting. Lilliana will save me something for a late lunch. My biggest concern now is how to see the kids. How do I reintroduce myself into their lives after disappearing for three months?

JOINT CUSTODY

Praise Goddess for the Blessings of the Twelve Steps. Daily practice beginning to live and breathe these seemingly simple, yet powerful spiritual principles help open a door for me in how to proceed with my divorce and most importantly how to retain joint custody of Bob and Kelly. Ram is not going to pay rent on the house beyond another month for getting me settled. I need to find a job and a place to live and demonstrate I am a fit custodial parent. Proving I have earning capability is one element of being fit to retain at least joint custody of Bob and Kelly.

My family seems to doubt my income-earning skills. Horse expertise doesn't pay the bills. I locate an apartment that, while not in a great location, isn't all bad. It is close enough that I can again take up my carpool duties. Kelly is now at Greenfields Country Day and Bob at St. Gregory's (now known as the Gregory School).

Those are treasured times for me, driving the kids to their after-school activities and then home to the Wendell house—listening to how they are experiencing school and their friends and how they feel about special after-school activities. It is emotionally painful to drop the kids off at my old home, now off-limits to me. No greeting of the dogs, no look-see checks of the remaining horses. The separation arrangement stipulates driving in, scoping out the landscape, seeing them safely in the door, and then leaving.

Luckily, I had the blessings of Jessie to call and a meeting to attend where I might bring up the topic [of gaining joint custody]. AA has meeting places in churches and storefronts all over the city, held daily and frequently. Ram was seeing someone. Deanna was a great deal younger than he—only seven years older than our son, Bob—and she provided stability and genuine affection in their "our Mom left us" home environment.

I insisted that Bob and Kelly both attend the weekly Alcoholism Council Youth Education and group session meetings for teens. Despite much grumbling from both kids and their dad, they complied. I picked them up from school and took them to the Alcoholism Council in central Tucson. Sometimes, Ram or Deanna picked them up.

My days were a juggling act; AA meetings, job hunting, and a course through the University of Arizona's College of Behavioral Sciences designed for adults trying to reenter the job market. Months of weekly meetings with lawyers to hammer out the financial formalities of our separation agreement and then, in June of 1983, our divorce—ironically, 20 years after our marriage in June of 1963, ate into job hunting. Ram and his lawyer were still questioning my status as a fit custodial parent. My psychological issues and track record of abandonment to go into treatment did not bode well. And I had yet to find a paying job.

After a particularly snarly procedure of psycho-social testing arranged by my lawyer to establish a case for my fitness as a parent, I remember descending the escalator of a high-rise building downtown and considering hopping a plane for Vegas. Just escape; no one would know if I drank. Instead, I passed the airport exit and made my way to the fairgrounds where the Arabian Horse Club was holding its annual spring-accredited horse show.

The first day I was at the treatment center, I called two people: Nancy McGibbon and Bazy Tankersley. I wanted both friends to know where I was and how to step in and help take care of the TROT horses and the Al-Marah horse I had at my Wendell home barn for training. They both expressed love, prayers, and support for getting me well and returning me as soon as possible to take up the reins of my responsibilities for TROT.

As if on autopilot, I now made my way through the exhibitors' entrance of the fairgrounds and circled the parking lot to the Al-Marah side of the stabling area. There I could see Mrs. T's familiar motor home, known affectionately as the TAO House parked alongside an Al-Marah trailer, I spotted Bazy's car and knew she was somewhere on the grounds—probably even showing herself. I made my way to the Al-Marah stalls and asked an apprentice where I might find Bazy. Bazy was just dismounting her horse, saw me standing in the aisle, smiled in delight, and said, "You are back!"
"

"Yes, I have been home a couple of weeks and working to get myself settled," I said, with a tremor in my voice. I was still shaken by the psychological testing. Giving her reins to an apprentice, she pulled me into her changing room, a curtained stall where we sat side by side on a tack trunk, in relative privacy. She put her arm on my shoulder—she, who is not a touchy-feely sort of person—and asked, "What's wrong?" I brought her up to date on the situation—in particular, my needing a job to prove I was a fit custodial parent so that I had a chance of getting joint custody in the divorce. That and the kids having a college education were my two primary concerns.

She thought for a moment and then said, "Look, I had to fire yet another farm secretary today. Apparently, I am a difficult boss. Why don't you come to the office Monday morning and I will have you slip into the job—at least until the agency can locate a replacement? You and your mom have secretaries. You know what it takes. And if after two weeks or a month, it isn't working out; at least you will have a job recommendation and a track record of income."

AL-MARAH

I turned to her in tears, gripping her in a hug. My gratitude was boundless. Neither of us had an inkling of what that next Monday morning and subsequent weeks and months and years would bring the two of us. But we did indeed know each other.

By the second day of work, I learned about Bazy's fetish for sharp pencils (from her newspaper years) and understand that in the office and in front of staff we are Mrs. T. and Barbara. Out and about on the farm and together socially we are Bazy and Barbara. She has discovered that thanks to my mom's insistence on me learning shorthand and typing skills in college, I am well prepared to step in and take her dictation of letters and articles for national magazines and to schedule her basic appointments.

I am adept at fielding phones. One line for Bazy's business, on which, if Bazy isn't in the office, calls are immediately forwarded to Helen Franklin, her administrative assistant for the farm. Another line for farm- and horse-related issues that I either forward directly to the barn staff involved, or to customer, training, breeding, or sale barn trainers or I take a message for Bazy to handle directly. Sometimes with the phones on hold, Helen and I hold a quick in-person conference as to what or whom, or how. I appear innately to require very little direction. Helen is in love with me and so is Weeta, the bookkeeper, who is also getting ready to retire.

Kelly showing Penny at a TROT schooling show.

BARBARA K. RECTOR

Bob showing Bintina in a TROT schooling show, circa 1974.

By Wednesday of that first week, Bazy has admitted that the office activity could get crazy. If I need a noon meeting instead of eating lunch in the lovely new office kitchen and porch eating area, then by all means get myself to the Alano club. Bazy tells me she has family members with alcohol problems as well as mental health issues. She feels like my personal cheering squad for recovery.

The other person on the office staff is Bill Freeman, the administrative assistant for the newly formed Arabian Horse Owners Foundation. Dave Trexler has his farm manager office in the breeding barn. The farm trainer, Joe Staley, has his office in the customer barn. By default, I handle the mail delivered daily in stacks and boxes, sorting mail for apprentices and farm staff into the kitchen mail shelves. I hand deliver to their desks the mail for Bazy, Weeta (bills & invoices), Helen (admin), and Bill (Arabian Foundation).

On Thursday, Bazy wants to know how I am feeling about the job. Did she pay me enough? With this question, we both realize we have not discussed payment. We go together into Weeta's office, the only one with a closed glass front door. (Bookkeepers have to concentrate to do payroll.) None of the farm has been computerized. We discover the job pays quite a bit more than my current budget; I am elated.

I take dictation in shorthand when Bazy is in the office. When she's at home, my workaholic friend dictates into a handheld tape recorder her correspondence, thoughts, and reminder memos to staff. These tapes are on my desk in the morning, and I put the Dictaphone plug in one ear to type transcriptions, leaving the other ear free to handle the phones. The work is exhilarating. Bazy is into all kinds of civic and horse world activities: implementing improvements and rehabs of the Desert Museum, reorganizing the habitats at the Tucson Zoo to create more humane shelters for captive animals, starting up the Arabian Horse Owners Foundation, and serving as a major force in the U.S. Arabian horse industry.

She is also developing her own cattle operation at her newly purchased Hat Ranch. Lo-

PORTALS TO MULTIDIMENSIONALITY

cated a short distance from Williams, Arizona, on the western slope of Bill Williams Mountain, this mostly state and federal forestland requires educated range management. Hat Ranch is a sizeable, privately owned piece of land for ranch headquarters, nestled within the Coconino Forest. Bazy holds seminars and forums there to further educate movers and shakers from environmental, cattle, and horse breeding associations as well as US Forest Service personnel.

I soon learn that Bazy has her finger in many pies, her influence extending even into the political realm. What follows is a true account of something that happened within the first several months of my employment as Bazy's farm secretary. The year is 1982.

Bazy had exchanged a significant amount of correspondence with her friend Armand Hammer, a businessman known for wheeling and dealing with the Russians. He had been on a stallion-buying mission to Russia, where he located an exceptional individual whose pedigree contained enough hybrid vigor from global outcrosses to benefit many US breeding programs. The problem was, several generations back in the dam line were the dreaded words "unknown." Good breeding records from the stud indicated progeny prized for the unique characteristics of the Arabian horse. The stallion was strongly prepotent for passing along these desirable characteristics to his offspring.

Best of all, the stallion and his progeny had passed the Russian state stud performance tests for conformation, riding, and free longe jumping and had been awarded a superior status. These performance and in-hand tests for specific breed vibrancy and inherited talent are required in Europe by the various state studs. Such testing was just entering consciousness here in the states; becoming required for both

The United States Arabian Horse Registry was denying Mr. Hammer's stallion approved breeding status without a certificate of authenticity from the Russian stud, and such a certificate added two million dollars to the US import fees (already considerable, on top of the stallion's original purchase price and airfare home to the states). Unless Congress could agree on a waiver to the rule because this particular stud's semen was likely to infuse for the better and greater good of the breed's many bloodlines in the US regardless of gene line emphasis. Mr. Hammer wasn't concerned about the money so much as the principle of the law denying full registry status and the benefits of overall outcrossed vigor being available to American breeders of the Arabian horse.

Mr. Hammer had reached the point of telling Bazy he would donate the two million to the Arabian Horse Registry if she could help him get the law changed, and rather quickly, as the stallion was scheduled to leave Russia the first of the following month. Now, for my part in this unfolding drama, Bazy comes into the office one afternoon with a plain white index card on which some penciled numbers are written. The numbers are in a line and appear to me to be some sort of code.

Bazy hands me the card and tells me it is a very private phone number. I'm to dial it and wait for the series of clicks and beeps until it is answered. I am sitting at my desk just outside her office door. Seated behind her desk, she can see me in profile facing the front door of the office as I work the phones or greet arriving customers. Bazy says to tell her when he is on the line and she'll pick up her phone.

I dial the numbers as instructed and hear a series of clicking beeps. Eventually, a very familiar, nationally known voice says, "Ronnie here. What does Bazy want now?"

"Ah, MR. PRESIDENT, here is Bazy to explain." I nod frantically at Bazy, pointing at the phone. She picks up. "Now, Ronnie, this will not be any trouble. You are going to like my plan…"

I sit stunned, watching Bazy and listening to her tell Ronald Reagan, then the president of the United States, her latest plan and her need for his help to improve the Arabian horse breed in this country. Two days later, a headline in the *Wall Street Journal* (there was a copy on my desk each morning) declares that Congress has approved an import tax waiver on Armand Hammer's Russian stallion. The Arabian Horse

Registry has extended reciprocity to the stallion's status as premiere with receipt of his performance records and those of his progeny.

Bazy is a natural, talented influencer. Being a part of her daily business life was teaching me organizational and critical thinking skills while capitalizing on my gift for teaching. Part of my growing area of influence was to continue offering late-morning riding lessons for the Al-Marah farm apprentices. I was also teaching Saturday lessons for TROT at Deon Kellner's Arabian training farm on Country Club Road, where the group had moved while I was in treatment.

Barbara and images from teaching.

Plans were underway for me to take a week off in the summer to help Kelly get to her riding and swim sleepover camp in Minnesota and at the same time to offer Bob, now sixteen, a much-lobbied-for chauffeuring experience, driving the three of us cross country in his newly acquired Jeep Cherokee. One of his dad's passions was to buy a safe, used might-be-needed vehicle for a family member.

My mom had suggested that I move out of the central Tucson apartment and pay her rent for the outside bedroom at MorningStar. She was ready to move home and not renew the lease on her Country Club rental. I would be quite close to work at Al-Marah and back in my old neighborhood for easier access to the kids. I would have my outdoor access and yet could go through the gallery and main house to get my meals and do laundry. Given Lilliana's cooking, this plan was not a hard sell.

TRAVELING

The trip to Minnesota with Bob and Kelly was fraught with delightful adventures, side trip stops, and my growing confidence, having an AA meeting list for the larger cities our trip took us through. I had the national office number in New York and only needed to call for directions for the location and time of a nearby meeting. I never actually used either but I did talk to Jessie, my sponsor, every other day or so. While we were at Gull Lake depositing Kelly at Camp Lake Hubert, Ram didn't want us to stay in what was legally still my cabin as well as his. I felt emotionally fragile about this, but by now I belonged to a professional women's AA support group and had been counseled by several AA buddies not to allow the situation or my feelings about Ram's behavior?] to hold me emotionally hostage. Ram's feelings and behaviors were his for him to make peace with.

Don and Marilyn Johannsen, who for twenty years had been my next-door neighbors at the Gull Lake cabin, suggested I stay in their cabin. They were not even there. I knew where the hidden key was, and they knew we would leave it spotless for their next weekend visit from Minneapolis. (Similarly, Ram didn't like me staying overnight with his parents when I was in Minneapolis, so I stayed next door with Betty Stinnette while the kids spent time with their grandparents and I went to an AA meeting.)

Once Kelly was in camp, Bob and I cleaned up the Johannsen cabin and covered his jeep to leave in 'our' cabin driveway for Ram's use later in the summer. Bob and I thoroughly explored the cabin garage as his dad wanted a full report on the condition of Ms. Greene, the '49

Cadillac I had driven at the University of Arizona and my first year of graduate school—now drained of fluid and stored in the garage. I had been her primary driver after Ram's grandmother, May, was no longer driving. Bob and I then flew home to Tucson.

Monday morning, I was back at work in the Al-Marah office and Bob, who was living at the Wendell house with his dad, began working at Eegee's, a local fast food restaurant in Tanque Verde. He had spent a hot afternoon dressed in green garbage bags, deep cleaning both bathrooms at Eegee's. He wanted to quit—not an option in the Morken or Rector families. Bob called later that week and said his dad had made a successful case for going on to college.

That trip with my son allowed us to re-bond and may have contributed to his role in one of my first after-'recovery and recovering,' meditation-induced, out-of-body journeys, which I know will sound a little woo-woo to some.

That first Christmas after being in treatment was hard. As negotiations for our separation agreement were drawing to a close, we had agreed upon joint custody as well as a college education for both kids, and I had moved from my rental to live in Mom's little guesthouse casita. I was working at Al-Marah, paying Mom rent on the casita, and participating in singles aftercare, while regularly attending AA meetings. I was earnestly working the steps, speaking with a sponsor, doing service work, and practicing daily prayers and meditation.

The kids were with me in the casita for a few days at Christmas time. We watched movies, took care of the horses now living in the pony paddock at MorningStar, and went up to the big house (Gammy's, as they called Mom), to enjoy her Christmas tree and Lilliana's cooking. Kelly and I did a trail ride on my mare, Rama, and Kelly's horse, Vargas, my gift to her for her fifteenth birthday. My gift to Kelly that year was easy to pick: a new double bridle for Vargas, as they were rapidly moving up the dressage levels.

After Christmas, the kids left to spend a week skiing with their dad and with my brother Walt, staying in Walt's Flagstaff home.

Ram was Walt's only brother and vice versa. There was a collective mutual agreement in our family that Ram and Walt were not divorcing. I wasn't invited and self-pity threatened to overwhelm me. Jessie and Bill (an aftercare counselor) both urged me to participate in more meetings and more being-of-service activities. I began work on the prison program—with a group of AA members who went weekly to the Wilmot prison to conduct an AA meeting.

I had felt emptiness around what to give Bob for Christmas. He had thrown his summer job money into the purchase of a hot little Mazda sports coupe. Kelly had inherited the green jeep, now painted white, so she might drive herself to Greenfields and then meet me at the barn after school. Bob was going to Arizona State University in the fall to study business and finance. On Christmas Eve, I had an inspiration. I had purchased a new-to-me silver grey Honda Prelude, Motor Trend Car of the Year, with a sunroof and a five-speed stick shift. Months earlier, as Bob had been inspecting it, he said to me, "Mom, you have an infinite capacity to surprise me."

As Kelly cooed over her double bridle and began gathering the olive oil, basin, and newspapers with which to begin oiling it, I told Bob of my idea. "You have always admired my car, and while it isn't new it has much less mileage than your own Mazda. I suggest we trade cars. "You are leaving town later than Dad and Kel, headed for Uncle Walt's and Shirley's. You wanted to see if your car was snow-worthy and you will have to purchase snow chains before you leave town." From the gleam in his eye, I sensed he was sold—with the caveat that his dad had to approve the title transfer, as he still held Bob's car loan.

"Mom you are doing the surprising thing again," he said. Everyone agreed that the trip to Flagstaff was a test run. Ram and Kelly were on the road early the next day, as a blizzard was scheduled to hit the mountains late that night. Bob promised to be at Uncle Walt's in time for late dinner. By mid-afternoon, I fell into such a funk that I lay on my four-poster bed, the one I got when I was seven living on the mountain in Charleston, West Virginia, and started alternating between deep breathing and prayers for their safe travel.

Suddenly, inexplicably, I am *in* the Honda Prelude, seated in the passenger seat next to Bob. Simultaneously, my awareness is such that I know there is a herd of elk ahead crossing the road in the blinding snow. The predicted blizzard has hit early and driving on the snow-slick mountain highway has become treacherous. The windshield wipers are working overtime and are unable to do an adequate job. "Pull off the road!" I shout to Bob. He has slowed considerably, has his hazard-warning blinking lights on; and his speed is down to a creep. Thank God for the snow chains on the tires gripping the road as he is making slow and steady progress. I see/sense/feel the three elk begin to gallop on a trajectory that will have them hitting Bob's car. These animals are like tanks; they can do considerable damage.

"Pull off the road!" I shout again. I've even pushed him on his right arm. He has no apparent awareness of me being there, so, taking a breath, I consciously slip into his body, take over the driving, and ease the car into a ditch just as the last largest elk lands with such a solid whoomph against the hood and windshield that the impact seems to kill him. The hit's force also moves the already angled front of the car further into the ditch. The Prelude windshield holds. Elk stunned by such incidents often regain consciousness and leap up and are on their way. Not this time.

Bob is hunched over the steering column, breathing deeply and trying not to vomit. The already snow-darkened sky is made considerably darker by the elk's giant presence across the windshield. If the animal does regain consciousness and leap up, will his hoof break through the glass and cause further danger and damage? Elk are known to be vicious if threatened.

Bob's breathing has slowed and he is looking at me still in the passenger seat, questioningly. "Mom, I smell you. Thank you." With that, I am popped back into my body, lying on my bed in the casita in Tucson.

In my awareness, I did note that Bob was located just a little north of milepost 149! I rouse myself, go to the phone, and call my brother Walt in Flagstaff. Ram answers. They have just arrived and he and Shirley are helping settle Kelly in the loft for their stay. "Honey, Bob's car has been hit by an elk. It's on the hood of the Honda in a ditch just north of milepost 149. He'll need to be towed and have help removing the elk. It appears dead."

Ram responds, "Now, honey, are you sure? Are you hallucinating again?" Hearing the concern in Ram's voice and being told it is me calling for him, my brother grabs the phone. "What's the deal, Sis?" I repeat to Walt that Bob's car is in a ditch with a huge elk on it, apparently dead; they are stuck and will need a tow out. I think the car is drivable. It is just a little north of milepost 149. I want Walt to take his big truck with bumper pull and help Bob out of the ditch. Walt says he is on his way and he will also call the Highway Patrol to meet them and help remove the elk. Walt affirms that he will have Bob call me when he is safely back home.

Later, as Ram is still questioning Walt as to the validity of Bob being a ditch, Walt says to Ram, "Look I've known her all my life. Frequently Barbara just knows things. Not logical makes no sense, and then generally always pans out." Hours later, Bob calls me from my brother's house. Uncle Walt and his dad did arrive in the big truck with a tow line to haul him out of the ditch. Within minutes of Walt's arrival, the highway patrol car pulled up with emergency lights whirling and helped pry the elk off the Honda.

Bob says to me, "Mom, I knew you were there. I could smell you. Thank you for helping me. And next time when you show up, could you please give me some warning? It's invasive not being aware of your presence."

I agree, and say that "this was just an unexpected result of my meditation practice. I love you". "I love you too, Mom", he replies. [1]

I have a life history of "knowing things." I

hoped that my increasing sensitivities and empathic skills would bloom into the ability to find TROT a new home property and contribute to Bazy's next big project for Al-Marah.

How is it I could continue to effectively function in the everyday three-dimensional world of the collective encultured reality of hard chairs and firm walls requiring doors? Let's go back to the spring of 1981, before my entering treatment in November of that year. Ram had moved out of the house and into an apartment and was taking the kids to Minnesota for their spring break and a visit to his parents in Minneapolis. My mom suggested I join her for her annual trip to Tecate in Mexico for refreshment and renewal.

On the second day in Mexico, after a hardy morning walk up the mountain for an ocean view and after a nourishing, delicious, organic vegetarian meal, I skipped my scheduled massage and returned to the familiar beauty of my casita for rest until my facial appointment, which was to be followed by a yoga class. Back in my room, I lay on my bed and began to have what I later learned were delirium tremors, a frightening hallucinating experience that felt like losing my mind. The treatment center would later tell me it was because I was not drinking my usual nightly quota of white wine. Mom came looking for me as I'd missed my massage; we had adjoining rooms.

She found me shaking, cold, and amid a violent episode resembling my lifelong incidents of night terrors. Gently, Mom awoke me and wrapped me in a blanket. I couldn't stop shaking. I am certain Mom was as terrified as I was, but she soothingly said we'd forget the afternoon program and go see her teacher, Indira Devi, after lunch. Her teacher? A visit to an ashram? This was a side of Mom I didn't know. Gradually, my shaking and coldness subsided and while Mom went to lunch I sat in the sun on our casita porch and semi-dozed.

Mom returned from lunch with news that our driver for the trip to the ashram would be arriving shortly. She suggested I wash my face and put on clean clothes. Mom dressed up and put on some makeup as if she were going to an event. She was; we were. From Tecate, it was only a short drive further into the hills to reach the ashram—a tiered, whitewashed stucco building with several cement steps leading up to a large wraparound porch surrounded by lush vegetation and glorious flower gardens.

A small, ancient Indian woman in a sari met us at the top of the porch steps and embraced Mom as a beloved friend. Mom introduced me as her eldest child, Barbara, who was suffering and required an audience with Indira. "Of course. Come this way. Mother will join us shortly."

We entered a lovely hall with a lofty ceiling and gently whirring ceiling fans. Deep oriental rugs and huge soft cushions were spread out on the floor near an altar where incense burned at the base of a statue of what I took to be the Buddha.

Our hostess set about serving us tea from a tray balanced on a small table near her cushion. Mom and I settled onto adjacent cushions, leaving a larger draped cushion on the other side of the tea table vacant. We made light conversation and then as I relax, listening to Mom and our hostess exchange gossipy updates, it gently dawns on me that Mom visits this ashram regularly and is considered a treasured member of their family.

I am busy scanning the large dark hall and various alcoves in which statues and figures are placed along the long walls. The only natural light comes through spaces between slats in the peaked roof. The environment is healing and soothing, partly from the fragrance of various blossoms floating in bowls of water around the statues. As my attention returns to Mom and our hostess, there is an extraordinary, lovely woman seated on the other cushion—maybe ancient, maybe young—who appears to glow

Mom and our hostess bow, with their hands in a prayer pose. I stare at the Beautiful Woman whose eyes penetrate my own. Mom says, "Welcome, Mother. Thank you for agreeing to this audience. My daughter Barbara is suffering."

Indira nods and leans forward from her cushion to embrace my mom in a hug. Mom has tears in her eyes. Our ancient hostess–has disappeared with the tea tray. On the table now is a tiny glass-stoppered bottle next to a shallow bowl in which a lotus blossom floats.

Indira reaches for both my hands. She gestures emphatically for me to move in close, gently tugging on my arms. I move closer, mesmerized by her eyes. Her glowing appears to radiate out to include me and Mom. Gently one of her hands scans my crossed-legs seated body, returning to the top of my head. Her other hand continues to hold my right hand. "Ah my child, you have grave difficulties and are caught between worlds of doing and knowing. You must learn to navigate between them more deftly. It won't be easy; portions will be very hard. I am guided to show you. You will remember as needed and know what and when you must act. Practice listening for and following guidance."

With these words and this touch, Indira withdraws her hands and turns to take the tiny glass bottle. She says it is vabutti, sacred ash from the Buddha. It has special properties. She upends the now unstopped bottle and has some ash on the end of her finger. With some chanting, she leans forward and places a dot of ash on my forehead between my eyebrows.

My brain explodes and I am whirled back to the Council of Light Beings where I am shown my life unfolding in slow motion, fast-forward frames. The Council is pleased with my actions in implementing TROT (therapeutic riding of Tucson). They are with me in my fight to retain joint custody of Bob and Kelly. I am to stay on the course guided always by LOVE. I am once again bathed in the warm pinkish glow of Universal Wisdom and Divine Intelligence of God. I am urged to take the high road with their father, a good and decent man. I am affirmed in my purpose of sharing the healing properties of horses for all phases of the human developing experience. And just as suddenly I am whisked back to being seated on the cushion with Mom and Indira.

As Indira leans forward to give the two of us a loving hug, the glowing presence continues to bathe us. And just as suddenly she is not there and is replaced by our ancient hostess, who helps us arise and walk to the entrance. She sees us down the steps to where our driver is waiting with the car. He has several plastic water bottles and urges us to drink them down on the return drive to Tecate.

Did that happen? I pepper Mom with questions. She tells me how my Dad in his search for sobriety found Indira and the ashram. He encouraged Mom to learn more about the Yogi practices. Mom met Indira at this same ashram; she in turn introduced Mom to Sai Babba after Dad's death. Mom affirms that the recall of my experience is mine. It will return as needed as my life unfolds.

Only twice since have I seen pictures of Indira Devi, the woman who glowed, who put the ash on my forehead, and embraced me and my Mom together. Once, during my first year in AA, when I joined a meeting group of women professionals, one of our members demanded that we read *Autobiography of a Yogi* by Paramhansa Yogananda. Thumbing through her hard copy, I saw a picture of the lovely Indira Devi, a beloved teacher of Yogananda, with a caption indicating that she left the planet in 1939.

Neither Mom nor I would have known her in the flesh. But she did know Mom. And she was there placing the ash on my forehead.

The other picture I saw was a group photo taken the year I spent five residential training days with Carolyn Resnik, the renowned "liberty horse" trainer. The photo was on the grand piano in Carolyn's living room and belonged to her mother, Pauline. The group was on the porch of the ashram I had visited in Tecate. According to Pauline, the photo depicted Indira with her most favored students. Astonished, I stared at the picture, and said, "Pauline! That's my Mom's teacher seated in the center, Indira Devi. I've met her! My Mom took me for a visit the spring before I entered treatment in the fall."

I said I had seen a photo of Indira Devi in a copy of the *Autobiography of a Yogi*. Pauline said the picture isn't in all editions. She called my attention to the section of the book where

Emerson is quoted: "That only which we have within, can we see without. If we meet no gods, it is because we harbor none." Further, he who imagines his animal nature to be his only reality is cut off from divine aspirations.

I had arrived late when I came to Carolyn's and my car had caught fire in their home's entryway. We three women had been baffled but had agreed to make the best of an unusual situation. My car was towed to the Subaru dealership for repair, and, to make the best of an unusual situation, I went with them to their local Whole Foods rather than do my grocery shopping as part of the residential protocol. In the ensuing discussion about women shopping and then preparing a meal together, we discovered many similarities.

Remarkably how my life in recovery has been traced and interwoven with spiritual truths and deep wisdom teachers, Carolyn's liberty training became available to me through A Course In Miracles friend, Franklin Levison, known then as the Maui Horse Whisper.

Later I will tell you the story of my student

training in liberty work with horses—of working with Carolyn and living in her lovely home with her mother, Pauline. For now suffice it to say that with my discovery of the photo of this precious woman in all our lives, our time together morphed into a strangely beautiful and powerful healing experience for the three of us. I went to bed that night recognizing there was a compelling purpose behind our enforced intimacy beyond the two scheduled nights for which I had signed up and paid good money. More to come; I get ahead of myself.

---

1. Bob's recollection: I was driving the Honda Prelude up to Flagstaff on I-17 by myself at night in winter, to meet you all at Walt & Shirley's cabin. The incident occurred on one of the uphill sections where semi trucks slow down and cars pass in the left lane. While passing a semi-truck on an uphill sweeping right hand curve, we came upon a group of javelina crossing the road in front of us. The semi hit the javelina in its lane, knocking one left in front of me. I braked hard for a second and immediately lifted off as I hit multiple javelina in my lane. They bounced left and right off the front bumper, but one went under the front

passenger wheel and dragged under the car a ways before the car rolled completely over it. The semi kept going and I stopped on the left shoulder. No one else was there. No other cars around. I walked back down the interstate with my pistol and a flashlight to see if any of the javelina were left on the freeway. There was only one laying on the road. It was dead and I dragged it over to the shoulder. The car's front plastic bumper had stress fracture lines, but was intact and firmly attached. The passenger side front wheel well and passenger side undercarriage had javelina skin, hair and blood, but were otherwise undamaged. I drove on and pulled off the interstate a few miles up at the next gas station exit. At the gas station I called the emergency number "911" from a payphone. They put me in touch with the Sheriff's department and I explained everything that happened, milepost, etc., and gave them my contact info. The Sheriff's department said they would send a patrol car up the freeway to check it out. I then called the cabin and told you all what happened. Then I drove the rest of the way up to Flagstaff and the cabin without incident. Dad had me get the alignment, suspension and brakes checked the next day. They were all fine. Also power washed the car the next day. Most important take-away: Hondas are like Timex watches, they can take a lick'n and keep on tick'n.

WORLD CRABBET SYMPOSIUM

We return to my life as Bazy's secretary.

Bazy, a natural teacher, had coached me into being helpful with the immense research required to validate the known pedigree of the Russian stallion's gene pool before agreeing to help Mr. Hammer get full approval with the Arabian Horse Registry. Bazy had discovered a predominance of what she labeled Crabbet Stud influence in these pedigrees half a world away. She had also become fascinated with the performance testing required of both mares and stallions for breed registry and full use as a state stud breeding animal.

These stallion tests are required for European horses of any breed to carry the designated signature brand of Westphalian or Hanoverian or Swedish Warmblood, et cetera. Bazy's fertile imagination hatched a major plan. She wanted to convene a global forum of Crabbet breeders, bringing together equine representatives from all over the world.

Kelly Rector Morken as office worker, World Crabbet Symposium

She wanted to persuade their owners to bring to a central place in the United States one or two of their prized breeding horses, mares or stallions, for a silent auction whereby the value of outcrossing and yet remaining true to line breeding principles would facilitate the retention of type vigor for both beauty and athleticism

Bazy was dreaming big. She wanted a living pedigree in the convention hall arena of stallions, their mares, and their progeny, along with demonstrations of their athleticism under saddle. They would demonstrate the various disciplines of riding in which Arabians were known to excel and be competitive: Jumping, Hunter under Saddle, Western Pleasure and Trail, Reining, Cutting, and Dressage.

She called her staff together to brainstorm. I took notes in shorthand and asked permission to tape-record the meetings. These meeting notes formed the basis of our strategy and led as I learned Bazy's tactical mind to more expansive plans: a World Symposium of Crabbet Breeders. She gave herself two years to bring this project to fruition. For me, watching Bazy work toward this ambitious goal was like getting PhD-level training in project development, operations planning, and communications and marketing.

On the first day, my task was to help Bazy draft and craft a major 'qualifications chart' on giant pieces of butcher paper taped to the wall in the copier and office supplies room. How did Bazy define a "Crabbet-bred horse" suitable for display and possible auction at the symposium? Bazy's lengthy phone calls and massive correspondence—this was in the days before computers—made clear her strong feelings about and broad interest in her massive undertaking.

To begin, we spent a year advertising in the major Arabian horse journals and corresponded with managers of various state studs throughout the world known to use Arabian blood in their breeding programs. Al-Marah's strength as a breeder of world-class Arabian horses meant that many of these countries in Europe, South America, and the Far East were our customers. Almost routinely, the farm would ship off a stallion or two with a small band of mares to these customer countries.

I learned early on how to help Helen Franklin make plane reservations for our horses and for an apprentice or two to accompany them. We also always had to make arrangements to follow the various quarantine rules and get vet checks to be sure animals leaving the United States were healthy. So as I embarked on collecting suitable horses for the silent auction I had some idea of the sheer paperwork and transport logistics involved.

As our first year of work concluded, we had yet to settle on a place in the States to hold the symposium. Bazy decided that I might need a larger office and a secretary of my own who could double as Bazy's private secretary. I was now the first lieutenant to Bazy on the Crabbet Symposium project. As preparation, she asked me to edit a Crabbet Symposium newsletter she was publishing to heighten excitement among her constituents. My title on the farm changed to Special Projects Director.

I was assigned to take over the private office

to the right of the entry door where Bill Freeman, executive director of the Arabian Horse Owners Foundation, had offices. (Bill had taken a leave of absence and the foundation had temporarily moved to Denver to share space with the Arabian Horse Registry.) Bazy liked that I had a window overlooking the main arena where the apprentices had their riding lessons; at least two days a week I continued to teach. Bazy helped me discover and hire Courtney to serve as Secretary for both Bazy and the Symposium project.

By 1983, I had been working a year and a half for Bazy. I now had a secretary and was the Director of Al-Marah Special Projects. In June of 1983, my divorce was final after twenty years of marriage to the day. Under the settlement, I had joint custody of the children and received child support from Ram until each became 18 years old. He also provided support for their college education. The shared custody kept Ram and me negotiating time with both kids together depending on school schedules and summer activities.

As my aftercare tenure wound down, I was grateful for the AA philosophy of practicing forgiveness—the idea that you are ultimately the source of your worst problems ("Stinking Thinking"). I was relatively poor economically speaking as compared to my old life and rich beyond belief in living my horse passion. Bob opted to live with his Dad at the house on Wendell Road; Kelly chose to live with me in a townhouse I had rented near our Jonas Irbinskas Training Stables barn.

RAMA AND VARGAS

Now a word about our two personal horses, RAMA and VARGAS, who figure so prominently in the development of my private experiential teaching business, Adventures In Awareness®.

The move from formal separation to divorce status accelerated one day when RAM had me visit the Wendell house to give me a check for the purchase of a new Oldsmobile Cutlass Supreme that he had ordered for me while I was still in treatment and he was still under the illusion that I would be home soon to take up the reins of our old life. I was seething. *What about my wishes? What if I don't want an Oldsmobile?*

Kelly showing Misty

RAM told me I was to go to the dealer where they had the car ready for pick up and give them the check. It was already made out to the local dealership for $10,000. Humph. I felt powerless and vowed to get myself to a meeting. I folded the check and put it in the pocket of my denim skirt. On the way, I stopped by Jonas's barn and saw him riding a gorgeous chestnut filly with a flaxen mane and tail. Surprised to see me, he trotted over, jumped down, and hugged me. "Who is this Beauty?" I asked.

"Oh, she's new. With a load, Heather drove in from Oklahoma. All registered quarter-horse youngsters. This filly is the oldest at four years and the most sensible. She is simply starting herself. Heather has a heck of a story about how this young mare kept her head on the freeway in New Mexico when the truck engine overheated on the big hill leading out of New Mexico and into Arizona."

I was walking around the mare inspecting her legs and her hindquarters. I'd already seen her deep chest girth and broad back, the well-set neck holding an exceptionally lovely head with a broad forehead, huge dark eyes, and perky ears big enough for me to know she was not likely to be easily startled or given to shying.

"She's adorable!"

Jonas told me to hop on her and take her for a test ride around the hunt field. He wanted to see how she looked under saddle. I was wearing a denim skirt and tennis shoes, so he told me to hike up the skirt and not use stirrups—he was already pulling them off the saddle. "You take her to the mounting stump. I want to see how she does with a stranger." He directed me to retrieve my hard hat from my tack trunk in the weathered wooden building nearby that served boarders such as me and Kelly.

Up on the flat stump of an old acorn tree, I vaulted lightly into the saddle and settled myself into Rama. When a horse fits; it just feels right from that first moment. Jonas was coaching me to pull myself together and move off briskly into a working walk. Forty minutes later I'd had a heavenly air-cushioned ride at walk, trot, and canter in both directions and one lap at a full-out gallop. Cooling her down, Jonas, now mounted himself, walked about the hunt field with us. "She seems to fit you," he said. "You looked good together. Easy."

Yes, that was how I was feeling. Easy. We belonged together.

"Well, don't get too excited," he said. "She's pricey. A beautiful mare like this is worth breeding. I want her for my stallion." Did I mention that Jonas was a master salesman and horse trader? He once had two lawyers in town owning and paying board on the same horse. The situation came to a head when both lawyers intended to ride their horses on the upcoming Los Caballeros Ride in northern California.

Hmmm, I murmur. We dismounted and I took Rama to the wash rack. She and I were both hot and dusty and in that mood of sweet tired exhaustion from mutual exertion. We both enjoyed the soothing cool spray of water. She glistened wetly. As I glide over her with the sweat scraper, I could truly see and form a picture of her superb conformation. Well, perhaps her back was a hair long; that would only make the flying changes come more easily. I already felt deep pride in heart ownership.

Jonas came over to tell me to go hand walk her about the stable yard, let her crop a little grass, and just be with her. He didn't have to ask twice. Crafty talented man—he was exceptional in the world of horses. He could ride competitively, teach, and train. It's rare to have a coach who excels in all three arts for developing a horse and rider team to their highest potential. I was a talented rider and teacher. But while I knew the inviolate horse rule that each time you engage with or handle a horse you are training the horse, conscious awareness of my training skill was not yet developed.

This awareness of training has come to me later in life as my body has shifted and changed with the passing years. I now ride less and teach and intentionally train more. Yes, I do still occasionally ride. At 14 hands, Princess Isabelle is a shorter version, of Rama who stood 16 hands of magnificence and fit perfectly in my then athletic slender body

Several months ago I told Izzy's owner that her walk was a 'take out your checkbook and purchase now' experience. Currently, I lease her to work with me in the *Presence of Horses* curriculum designed to capitalize on AIA's Invitational Approach. *Adventures In Awareness* is an experiential education program offering elders opportunities to make a friend of a horse and in the process discover more about themselves in this, the final phase of their life's journey.

As I walked about the stable yard with Rama cropping grass, Heather joined me to tell the story of her trip hauling five fillies and one colt, just gelded, home from an Oklahoma ranch. The youngsters, all under four years, were nestled into her six-horse stock trailer. They had been started—meaning they could be led by a halter and knew how to pick up their hooves for trims and cleaning. They had been handled and for the most part, had suitable ground manners when worked in hand on the halter.

She had been making good time on the long haul trip when their ancient dually truck (a pickup with a double set of tires) coughed and sputtered up the big hill in New Mexico just before the Arizona border. I knew this long stretch of Interstate 10, straight up from the lowland desert to the beginnings of mountain foothills—from sea level to 1,700 feet.

Heather noticed that the truck's temperature was alarming and as the engine began to blow smoke from the hood she found a wide shoulder with a guard rail to safely pull off the highway. The truck and loaded trailer were rocked by the passing semi-dual trailer rigs that were often stacked up in a line chugging up the hill, so she said a short prayer such as "Lord, please keep us all safe" and got out of the truck to set her safety cones and turn on some flares. After nearly an hour no one had stopped to help. This was before cell phones and those handy emergency call phones on the roadways.

It was the heated part of the day, with high sun and baking temperatures. She had enough water on board to give half a bucket to each horse and realized that if no one saw her watering the horses stopped, she was in deep trouble. With huge sighs and out loud prayers to keep both her and the horses calm, she unloaded each one and tied them in the blessed shade of the off-highway side of the trailer.

From her one overnight, sleeping in the truck at mid-journey Texas fairgrounds, she knew Rama was the easiest loader and served as the little band's alpha. Rama appeared to agree with Heather's voiced-out-loud plan to make reins hooked to side metal keepers of halter using an extra lead line. Bringing Rama over alongside the truck's fender, she used the fender to slide onto Rama's broad comfortable back. She had considered taking the colt first. She had purchased him as her future three-day horse. But the colt was still sore from his recent gelding; he continued with the stud behaviors of a horse meant to be breeding and undoubtedly still carried those hormones in his roaring system. (Many freshly gelded colts have been known to successfully impregnate a mare.)

Giving them both a moment, as heavy-duty cross-country freight tractor and trailer rigs speeded by; Heather did some deep breathing 'pre on course' to chase away the jitters and opened to feeling Rama. Good solid steady sensible Rama, who she didn't know for certain had ever been backed by a rider before. Rama felt very green and very willing with her ears flicking back to Heather and then forward and around to scan the environment.

"Well, girl, it's back down the highway's shoulder for us, against traffic, to the gas station I can barely see in the distance."

With a clear goal and vision, Heather urged Rama to a rhythmical walk. Step by step they fell into a pattern of Heather breathing and praising Rama for being such a solid sensible girl. Nearly an hour later, with only the slightest kerfuffle, the pair rode into the gas station requesting help.

A courtly motorist in a handy pickup truck volunteered to carry the several jugs of water and allow Heather to ride in the truck bed holding Rama's reins reconfigured to a halter lead line. He kept to the white line of the highway shoulder with his hazard warning blinkers on as Rama obligingly jogged along on the sandy dirt. While the gentleman cowboy wrestled with the truck's engine, Heather sponged off Rama and gave water to the waiting horses, which had had a nice doze. There were no signs of pullbacks on the ropes and there was no churned-up dirt from uneasy hooves.

Heather finished her tale with the insight that if the rest of the load were like Rama, all of them registered American Quarter Horses with Rama's demonstrated sensible in a-pinch nature, pliable disposition, and heart and desire to get the job done—well, that kind of versatility had her dreaming of breeding more. She had watched Rama's trot up the hill, she said, and believed that with her confirmation she had the talent to reach the seriously higher levels of dressage. And Heather was right. Rama and I with the help of Jonas worked our way up the training scale to reach and show successfully up to the *Prix St.* Georges—the first level of FEI. Federation Equestrienne International

It would take us decades to build our relationship, become a competitive team of dance partners, birth three awesome babies (one colt, Bill W, paid my way to graduate school), work and teach TROT independent riders ready to canter and help the TROT Instructors learn long lining skills for the outpatient Hippotherapy Clinic. Later Rama moved with me to Prescott, Arizona, to live at the Episcopal Retreat Center and help kids and adults in the developing Adventures In Awareness program.

"Heather, Jonas said she's pricey. Are you going to sell her?" I ask.

"Yes, with some restrictions," she replies. "We want to retain two breeding covers for Alahi. That will bring down her price somewhat."

"Well, how pricey?" I ask again.

"Probably at least ten thousand dollars cash," she responds.

What do you suppose the amount is written on the somewhat sweat-dampened check that is now burning a hole in my pocket? "I don't suppose you would take a counter sighed third-party check, would you?" I tell Heather about the Oldsmobile Cutlass Supreme. "Let's get Jonas and go to lunch," says Heather. "You'll need to call your lawyer to see if that is even legal."

I go into their house to use the phone while Heather speaks to Jonas. Yes, it's legal, I just have to tell Ram what I'm doing. Bill suggests I wait until Jonas deposits the check at the bank and that I go with him.

That phone call to Ram wasn't pretty. It cemented according to him any and all opportunity for any kind of restoration of our marriage. At any given time over the two years of our separation, he had made noises about a possible reconciliation. I was susceptible to his influence. I was still a young woman who had never expected to not be married. The emotional trauma of divorce, my alcoholism recovery an active process day by day, and my fragile just beginning to bloom sense of self as a professional woman ...I had been waffling. I did love him. It simply wasn't good for my health to be married to him.

Holding that line with Ram and recognizing I wanted and needed Rama and the independent assertive 'I can do and achieve anything' spirit that riding her gave me served to snap me out of the spiral into depression I had started to enter. We went to lunch and made the deal, recording specifics on paper napkins for Bill Tinney to transcribe into a contract.

Jonas had wanted the two breeding covers training and boarding with him for at least two years, and in my commitment to ride and work Rama a minimum of four days a week, I had to agree to visit her at the barn every day unless I was sick. If I didn't make it, then Kelly had to be willing to come and see Rama. All of his boarded horses had owners who visited daily, or Jonas knew the reason why. Too many lapses and you were asked to leave. I had her registration papers signed over to me.

Kelly's birthday was approaching; she would be fifteen years old. Mature and responsible, she had followed through on her agreement to see to Rama when I could not make it to the barn. The bus from GreenFields Country Day School would drop her at Jonas's and I would collect her once I was off work. Our efforts at Bazy's were intensifying as we moved into the second planning year of the World Symposium on Crabbet Horses.

Kelly had a black quarter-horse-type mare, Decka Delight. I once rode her and found her anything but, and Kelly loved her. I felt she was a full-out pill and no one ought to be required to ride her; Kelly and Deli cleaned up at the local shows. They were a very competitive pair. Then one day Jonas remarked to me that Kelly's skills and talents had outgrown the mare. He wanted me to look around with him for a more suitable horse, capable of going the distance—a three-day horse for Kelly – a horse capable of higher levels.

Coincidently, he had a customer interested in purchasing Deli and breeding her. (Again, the master horse trader.) He said this customer was coming in next week and wanted to take Deli back to his New Mexico ranch to have in his brood band. While we looked around for Kelly's next horse, he would put her to work under Heather, who schooled the sale prospects. It would be good practice for Kelly to ride and help train different horses.

I was receptive to the idea. I told Jonas that the whole plan was up to Kelly. He lost no time telling Kelly as we were leaving the next afternoon that he had a man from New Mexico arriving sometime the next week that had evidenced interest in purchasing Kelly's horse Deli for his broodmare band. "Oh, I don't know," she tells me in the car.

"Well, no pressure," I respond. "It would up your skill base to be riding with Heather and helping her to train the young sales prospects. Think about it. Let's meet this rancher and get a feel for what our hearts say."

Several weeks go by and one day a huge rig pulls into the stable yard. The ramp comes down and out struts a magnificent liver chestnut gelding. He looks around curiously, shakes himself, snorts, and strides forward with the handler to look for Jonas. Kelly and I are both drooling. We turn as one unit to follow the man and the horse and watch the movement of the horse's walk, especially his overstep— whereby ideally a hind hoof hits the dirt several inches ahead of the mark left in the sand by the same side front hoof.

The massive liver chestnut appears to have a perfect walk. Something very rare; it looks like a 10, the score given in dressage for the extended walk across the diagonal that carries a multiple of 2. The handler greets Jonas, who directs him to turn the horse out in the large schooling arena to get his travel kinks out. The horse has attracted the attention of several other boarders who huddle with us, observing the horse's movement. He is a stunning mover.

Vargas is his name, Jonas tells the observing crowd. He is 17.2 hands high, an above-average height on a horse. We watch him athletically drop to the ground and roll, flopping over from side to side several times—like a great land whale. Then he springs up and shakes himself to dig in his hindquarters and take off at speed, racing around the arena. He even trots up the bank jump and gracefully soars off the three-foot drop fence to land bucking. Eventually, he slows to an elegant cadenced trot, cooling himself out.

A stunning horse, I'm thinking. Jonas says he's been purchased by a customer and is here to learn his manners and get some serious starting properly green (walk trot canter) training. Vargas is three years old, barely grown for his warmblood/thoroughbred gene pool. His real work will begin after his knee plates are closed, likely in three-to-four years, says Jonas.

As it happens, the man riding shotgun in the rig is also the breeder interested in Kelly's Decka Delight. We meet him and see him at the barn over the next couple of days. Heather hasn't waited for Kelly to decide to let Deli go; rather, she has given her two green prospects of a different type and feel to school during her lessons.

Kelly's skill base has improved by leaps and she has decided the world holds other promising horses. It feels good to know that Deli would go to pasture and help produce magnificent specimens such as the amazing chestnut colt, Vargas. At the end of the week, Deli boards the big travel rig to head for her new home in New Mexico.

And now Kelly's fifteenth birthday is approaching. Heather approaches me to begin negotiations with Jonas for the purchase of Vargas. The original buyer has decided Vargas is too much horse for his pleasure trail aspirations. He is a perfect three-day horse for a solid seated rider with similar interests and desires. Heather believes Kelly and Vargas to be a suitable pair and Jonas agrees.

We begin our talks with what ifs and have reached the point where I had a Dodge Ram dually truck, very ancient with a cab over camper that had hauled our four-horse stock trailer to many out-of-state competitions. My divorce settlement has been rolling along and includes ten acres in an undeveloped area of Sonoita.

My practical mom, who feels Vargas belongs in our herd with Rama, says, "How are you going to pay the taxes on the ten acres anyway?"

She sees two horses as manageable and if my economic status gets shakier they could live in the back acreage of MorningStar's pony paddock.

The use of an appreciating asset to purchase a depreciating asset further separates Ram from the world I live in. He doesn't understand my passion for horses and how important they are in developing my relationship with sobriety and my children, who are becoming young adults. An agreeable trade is reached and Vargas belongs to Kelly and us.

I plan to have Mom and my friend Tom stand by to take photos at the barn as Kelly walks from the GreenFields van into the stable yard. As she wonders out loud what all of us are doing, I hand her a huge ball of twine with instructions to follow the route the twine takes her. Heather and Jonas appear along with Kelly's barn friend Leah to watch her track the twine.

First to our tack room for a new very large leather halter, then to a tree where there is an extra lead line (all leather) next to Rama's stall, and then finally, circuitously to the large premier wooden stall that houses Vargas. As Kelly looks ahead and sees the line end at his door latch, she began crying and laughing and going "No way!"

"Yes, way. Happy birthday! Now he's yours if it works out." Kelly and Vargas enjoyed a stellar career over the years, reaching twelfth in the nation in all breeds at second-level dressage.

TRAVELING

About the time we bought Vargas, my work with Bazy on the first world symposium of Crabbet horses took me away from Arizona. Early in the second year of our planned campaign, I flew to Denver to see if the large coliseum for the Denver Livestock Show would suit our needs.

We needed a centrally located city where monetary exchanges were easy, with a downtown accustomed to livestock moving through its streets, and with good nearby comfortable hotels. As I toured the livestock pavilion with the manager it quickly became apparent that the huge main arena was much too large. Our vision was for an intimate extended family gathering, tea garden, and living pedigree along with discipline demonstrations of the horses under saddle – culminating in the final day of the silent auction.

Obligingly the manager told me that across the street they still had the main bowl building of the first livestock show. It had ancient but adequate stalls and a second-floor exhibitor space that might be transformed into a tea garden. He zipped me over in his gator (a heavy-duty golf cart) and I knew almost immediately that it was perfect. The ancient building in the shape of an elongated bowl had a skylight illuminating what might otherwise have been a gloomy interior.

Inside, the floor was ringed by bleachers. Best of all, the interior colors were Al-Marah's yellow and green. The manager told me they intended to repaint as the place was functional and shabby.

"Yes, do repaint", I said, but keep these same colors. The stalls in the adjacent barn building were way too dark and gloomy. There was no budget for repainting and none for the second-floor exhibit space.

I called Bazy and reported my findings. She got on the phone to negotiate the price with the manager and the finance person who had joined us. The site was secured and I was off to the local Denver Hotel to book rooms for our international guests, who are becoming quite a crowd. I remained for a week to speak with the Denver livestock manager about our Sunday auction of Crabbet horses. To my dismay, I learned that Colorado was a dry state, which meant that on Sundays there could be no sales of alcohol and no gambling—and our auction was classified as gambling!

As you might guess, Bazy got on the line with the governor and negotiated a waiver, persuading him that our auction would hugely benefit the horse industry through an infusion of a premium international gene pool. In no time our World Crabbett Symposium was a nonprofit enterprise. We would hold a private auction with only guests as participants; the bids would be displayed on an electronic tote board at the end of the arena. Our plans were falling into place.

Kelly's spring break was at the same time as the symposium and she agreed to be my roommate and help out. She would fly to Denver the day before the opening night gala when we would raffle off our 'million dollars' mare, Miss Moneypenny. (Her presentation on the red carpet of the hotel ballroom was a royal success. She had her sparkle stall in the center of the ballroom.)

The week before the Symposium, Bazy and Helen Franklin set out to drive to Denver. Following them in the van were Courtney, me, and a newly hired assistant to the assistant, Carol. We were driving Tank's huge Cadillac convertible with his gas credit card in the glove compartment. Bazy had made reservations for us at the Inn of the Gods in Santa Fe. We all had a lovely dinner and retired to our elegant rooms.

The next morning, after retrieving the bill under my door, I went in search of Helen and Bazy. Courtney and Carol had shared the room adjoining mine but Bazy had the checkbook. The front desk informed me that Bazy and Helen had left in the night. What? I called Tank at home in Tucson. Yes, he knew Bazy and Helen were on their way back home. Bazy had had an attack of agoraphobia and needed to be in her place.

How would I handle the giant Inn of the Gods hotel bill? How would I continue to Denver to register at a hotel with several floors of booked rooms? I was breathing deeply, trying not to panic. Tank asked what credit cards I had. Well, none. His Mobile gas card in the glove compartment was good only for gas. I did still have a Mastercard in my former married name, Barbara R Morken. Ram insisted I keep it in case of emergency.

"This is somewhat of an emergency", said Tank.

. I would need to call Ram and warn him, I said—but while the Mastercard might get us out of the Inn and on the road to Denver with a meal, I doubted it would cover the $28,000 in down payments on the rooms at the Denver hotel. Tank said he would call Ram after we spoke to verify that once the banks opened for business, he would transfer funds to upgrade the Mastercard I was carrying.

I called Ram at about 5:30 am Tucson time.

"What is it now, honey?" He asked.

(Mornings were never good for Ram.) I told him that Tank would be calling shortly to sort out the need for using his card. Ram insisted I retain that emergency, backup, credit card for a good five years after our divorce; I had several occasions to use it, always calling Ram first.

Courtney drove to Denver with Carol in the navigator seat. I sat in the back with my giant daytimer and planning guide, figuring out how to cover the slots now vacated by Bazy and Helen. Checking into the Denver hotel went without a hitch. When I was asked, "Is there anything else we can do to help you?" I asked if they had an AA meeting schedule. The concierge lifted his head and said he would take me to his home meeting nearby if I could wait till seven. Ah, the amazing support of the twelve-step program. Courtney decided she wanted to come with us.

From my room, I called Bazy, who was truly heartsick at bailing on this, feature project. What could she do to support me? I told her about the concierge taking me and Courtney to an AA meeting nearby. Kelly will be there late tomorrow. Do you want your sponsor? Ah, that's an excellent idea.

Jessie's health didn't allow her to fly. She suggested I call Bill, my aftercare counselor. Bill already had an open schedule as it was his son Will's Spring break and they had intended to play golf and more golf. Bill could hear in my voice frantic panic. I explained my situation. I was feeling the need for close at hand 12 Step support to get through the next ten days. Jessie had suggested I call him. Bazy would buy plane tickets, hotel double rooms, and meals. "OK, we'll be there tomorrow", he said.

When Kelly and Will were not out running errands for the crew rehabbing and painting the stalls and crafting the second-floor tea garden, they worked in the office helping with registration and money exchange.

Mr. Player, Bazy's CPA arrived from Maryland to handle the finances. Bazy's son, Mark Miller, arrived with his truckload of Micanopy Farm horses to organize the families of living pedigree. Mark had a new computer; it influenced the staff's attitude on ease of scheduling and organization.

Bill took over supervising the office and schedules and tying in the communications, which were handheld radios—this was before cell phones. Bazy suggested, not for the first time, that I 'be' her and act as the hostess meeting and greeting our hundreds of guests, making sure they had what they needed, especially for their horses.

To this day it is a tribute to the talented people Bazy attracted to her projects that our symposium was such a smashing success. It was clear that Al-Marah customers considered themselves family and pitched in to do what was required to produce our show. The living pedigree was awesome and contributed a great deal to the knowledge base of breeding principles and the significance of conformation to a horse's function in a particular discipline be it dressage, hunter/jumper, western pleasure, trail, reining, and cutting.

Bazy's decorator friend Marty Lynch flew up to manage the tea garden transformation and help with recordings of old timers in the field telling their stories of special horses in their lives. We produced a remarkable historical document that later became a collector's item. The hardest to manage was the dang cows. They were constantly getting loose, breaking out of their pens, and causing general mayhem.

The project evolved over the years into every other year gathering somewhere in the central U.S.

TROT

THERAPEUTIC RIDING OF TUCSON

Once back at the farm, I eased into more full-time training and teaching for TROT. Therapeutic Riding of Tucson, Inc. was again in need of a new—a more permanent—home. We had been 'camping' fully operational on borrowed acreage owned by Bob Cote, the owner of the Tanque Verde Guest Ranch. Bob's large herd of dude horses traveled summers to Minnesota to work at his kid's camps, Camp Lake Hubert for Girls and Camp Lincoln for Boys.

Bob was a tremendously generous soul who adored horses and believed in TROT's vision and mission of helping challenged kids and adults enjoy the benefits of riding a horse. He suggested a potential home somewhere along Woodland Road in the Tanque Verde area. I knew the ground as my mare Rama and I frequently rode the trails around that neighborhood after a schooling session with Jonas.

8920 E. Woodland Road was an abandoned private home owned by a local physician who kept cattle. It had been condemned by Flood Plain to serve as a dyke for the rest of the pricey homes in the neighborhood. As Rama and I purposefully scouted the land and the buildings, I developed my thrill bumps, and tingles up my spine signaling, "AHAA…this is it. TROT's new home!"

Nancy McGibbon and I went into conference with Bazy, who suggested we write a project grant proposal to persuade the Pima County Board of Supervisors and the Flood Plain Control authority to allow us to lease this abandoned home along Woodland Road to serve as TROT's permanent home. Blessings for Bazy and her political acumen; she counseled us to touch base with the Woodland Road neighbors and get them on board with our plan.

We proposed to acquire a permanent home on lease to TROT from the City's Mayor and Council. Tucson was in process of annexing that portion of Woodland Road as part of floodplain management. The 25-acre piece of property was recently condemned to serve as a dike for the rest of the neighborhood. It stood at the headwaters of the Pantano Wash, which in flooding times—every one hundred years – became a raging river. More about flood issues in Rama's Magic story.

As we were designing and writing our grant proposal, we involved the Pima County Parks and Recreation Department as they had input and control of the river bank's vegetation and that of the land itself; badly in need of trees. Trees are needed on the property as their roots would reinforce and stabilize the flood plain's sandy earth. Bazy and my mom embarked on a series of dinner parties designed to acquaint the neighbors and the community with our proposed use of what had become public property.

PORTALS TO MULTIDIMENSIONALITY

Once Pima County, Flood Plain, City Parks, and Recreation, and the mayor and town council had all voted their approval, we had a new home at 8920 E. Woodland Road. Bazy had suggested that the TROT Board hire me full-time to direct programs at our new home, be the lead instructor of therapeutic riding lessons, and train and teach the horses and volunteers how to offer services.

Nancy became the clinical director handling the medical screenings and offering her physical therapy expertise as we selected mounting and adaptive equipment. I found an AA buddy and her traveling salesman husband willing to live in the onsite caretaker cottage and take care of our horses morning, noon, and night.

With Kelly now in college, Mom agreed to let me move home to MorningStar and live in the caretaker cottage, which was not quite a five-minute drive from TROT's new home. We were flooded with volunteers. I discovered that I loved teaching. Something mystical and mysterious happened to all of us each time we put a full treatment team together or mounted a full group lesson of six to eight riders in our large arena.

Saturdays were reserved for volunteer lessons and those who excelled in basic walk trot and canter were invited to join the Sunday wash trail ride. That gave both humans and horses refreshment and vitality exploring the magical Bosque groves of trees and vines in the riparian riverbed environment.

For many months in the spring of 1988, I had a member of a major media outlet, print, TV, and radio filming our lessons and reporting on our operations. Even today for Saturday morning cartoon hour there will be me and our TROT family teaching a lesson on some PBS station somewhere around the globe. But in the fourth year of this amazing avocation, I was reaching burnout. We were owned by the community, and I was becoming grumpy. Later, in graduate school, I would learn that this was known as compassion fatigue.

Some friends in my professional woman's AA group had encouraged my involvement in a very progressive local Methodist Church, St.

Francis in the Foothills. I admired David Wilkinson's willingness to explore the depths of faith and spirituality outside the boundaries of accepted thought and culture. David had invited Matthew Fox, the Catholic priest who had recently been silenced by the Pope and threatened with ex-communication, to visit our church in Tucson

Dr. Fox's Creation Centered Spirituality spoke to my soul. *A Course In Miracles* had recently crossed my path. I read the main text one night and felt rested the next day, despite having no sleep. A seed was growing within me. I also felt a growing desire to visit and study with Jerry Jampolsky, a Bay area psychiatrist and one of the publishers of *A Course in Miracles.* Jerry's center for children dealing with early death offered classes and counseling for families whose children faced impending death; there were internships available for qualifying students.

And my soul knew there was no death. My angst and grumpiness could be signaling that I needed to work more on integrating my near-death experience. Both David and Mathew suggested I visit the College of the Holy Names (later renamed Holy Names University) in Oakland and take a semester's certificate study program in Creation-Centered Spirituality.

I might also volunteer with Dr. Jampolsky and his Center for Attitudinal Healing in nearby Tiburon while taking coursework for the master's program in spiritual psychology in Oakland. Accustomed to driving in the wide open spaces of the desert, I did not regard the distance around the bay from Oakland to Tiburon as much of a commute. The application for the certificate program at Holy Names was the Barnum and Bailey aptitude test for clowns, an employment screening test, plus an essay on personal purpose. I worked a week on the application and essay and sent it off with my fingers crossed.

Miracle of miracles, I was accepted for the fall semester of the certificate program. The work of replacing me at TROT began in earnest. I sold Rama's second colt, Bill W, to a local endurance race rider. TROT agreed to lease Rama for work in their independent riders program. Her advanced training in dressage and willingness to a long line made her valuable for teaching the instructor's mastery of the art of long reining thereby providing a steadier support platform for unbalanced and challenged riders.

Vargas had pulled up lame in a California competition and was later diagnosed with an osteoarthritic condition called high ringbone. Too old to be a surgical candidate for joint fusion, he required a year of turnout on pasture—time out from riding or work to allow his joint to fuse on its own. Judy Meade's race trainer husband Sonny invited Vargas to rehab in the grass paddock behind his house. The two would share a beer in the evenings and look over the crop of mares in Sonny's east paddock.

Bob was in Phoenix studying finance at Arizona State University for a degree in Business while working as an apartment manager for his lodgings. Kelly had just returned from a year of living and working with her Aunt Shirley in Germany, as a caregiver to her young cousins,

Wendy and Josh. At the same time, she was studying with Johann Hintermann, a renowned dressage trainer who coached at the Olympic level--while also earning riding lessons from the barn's advanced students. She was now enrolled at Northern Arizona University, studying social work in Flagstaff

In preparation for my move to San Francisco and the Bay area, TROT hired three new people to do what I had been doing. It was good for me to take time out and turn over the reins of teaching, training, and scheduling to others.

By this time I was also TROT's development director, writing funding grants—a nearly full-time position. I was budgeted fairly tightly and my mom offered to help by picking up my dorm and meal expenses at Holy Names University in Oakland. Because of my background at TROT, the Attitudinal Healing Center offered me a stipend to co-facilitate grief groups for parents. Dr. Jampolsky and his son Lee would serve as my supervising mentors.

I planned to drive from Tucson to Oakland and Holy Names; I wanted to take my saddle and riding gear. It was time to turn in Bob's Nissan (which I'd swapped for at Christmas) and acquire a new SUV for the two-day journey. The money I got from selling Rama's last colt, facilitated the down payment on a new Isuzu Trooper. I called her Trolley, for the San Francisco area. Several years later the kids at Sierra Tucson Adolescent Care would think I ran drugs as my Trooper had a built-in first-edition analog portable phone—Mom's gift for graduating from graduate school—for long-haul journeys to Flagstaff in early September of 1990.

In mid-August of 1988, having secured TROT a permanent home at 8920 E. Woodland Road, and the staff to take my place with an on-site couple caring for the horses, I set off on an amazing adventure.

Listening to Carolyn Myss's tapes on spiritual practice as I drove, I arrived at the College of the Holy Names in two days. I settled into my third-floor dorm room, adjusting to the living space being both co-ed and richly inhabited by nuns and clergy as well as my classmates

—some, like me, signed up for a half-year certification semester, but many enrolled in the full graduate program.

Mathew Fox would not be teaching classes as he had been recently silenced by the Pope. He would appear weekly for our discussion and dialogue class, where the entire year's class met as a community for three hours of collective learning in creation-centered spirituality. My first justice advocacy activity was supporting the nuns in their whale watching census of whales in the Bay area—noting especially the moms and babies.

Meeting with my academic advisor, we reviewed her suggestions for my classes. In Artistic Expression, I would learn the concepts and principles of drawing "con su permiso" (a Spanish phrase meaning "with your permission"), a process I later incorporated into my energetic Con Su Permiso interaction with horses. In Vocal Expression I focused on breath development and diaphragm strength; I remain unable to carry a tune. I studied African dance and rituals in the gym with Luisah le Teish an ordained priestess of Oshun in the Yoruba Lucumi (African) tradition. My Shamanic Studies were with StarHawke (whom the nuns called in to help pray for the school during a major earthquake in November 1989, 7.8 on the Richter scale.

My favorite course—Dream Tending with Jeremy Taylor—would prove pivotal in helping me integrate my near-death experience. For example, at my very first breakfast in the college cafeteria before going to classes, I was carrying my food-laden tray and was flagged by a friendly nun from my floor. I sat down next to her and looked up to see staring back from across the table a fabulously handsome man straight out of my recurring dreams of the past years. His piercing blue eyes met my grey-green and simultaneously we said, "Don't I know you?" We spent that breakfast bantering about where we were from, what we were doing there, and what our first class was. It is possible we did somehow recognize each other.

Billy Holliday, also born in 1942, lived all his life in Myrtle Beach where my family vacationed for years. We both knew and had spent summers riding on the beach merry-go-round, where if you caught the ring you might earn an extra ride. Billy knew of Miss Manning's boarding house where we stayed and counted as a life friend Mackie, who taught me and my siblings how to crab fish. I became the older woman in Billy's life by two months. He was in his final semester and would graduate in the spring to return home to his fiancée Harriett, and his duties as North Carolina Agricultural Commissioner.

The others at the table listened in fascination as Billy had been among them for almost a year and a half, and I had learned more about this handsome loner from a major tobacco family in the forty-five minutes of our meal than had been previous public knowledge. And an odd fact emerged: His room in the dorm on the second floor was exactly below my own on the third floor.

Our first class that Monday morning was the same: Jeremy Taylor's Dream Tending. In most of these classes we were seated in a circle, in desks with a writing surface on the side—desks easily moved around. We walked in still bantering—which would turn to mild flirting before the week was up.

Jeremy Taylor easily became my favorite teacher with his remarkable reach on the topic of dreams and on practical applications for recalling the barest snippet of a dream's feel, color, and mood. How you felt when you awoke and the significance of paying attention—intent on learning from your dream life. We used as a text his seminal work, *Where People Fly and Water Runs Uphill*.

Billy and I also had an evening class together: the weekly Creation Centered Spirituality, for which the texts were Mathew Fox's books *Via Negative, Via Creative* and those of his favorite mentors: John of the Cross, Teresa of Ávila, and Hildegarde de Bingen. During the break, Billy and I would make our way to the nun's hilltop gardens overlooking the Bay, with Oakland's sparkling city lights in the foreground and those of San Francisco in the background. We would just stand next to each other, quietly being, among the nuns' fragrant flowers.

The chairs for this class were set in a semi-circle with the school's acting head, Professor John Conglon, filling in for Mathew Fox. I invariably took the seat furthest left on the half-moon circle, and Billy invariably took the seat at the other end, so we were facing each other, with the teacher in the middle. In this triangle, the three of us fell into amazing critical-thinking dialogues.

Walking back to the dorm that first night, I told Billy that the heated triangular discussion we had with the teacher reminded me of a twelve-step program I belonged to, with its motto "Experience, Strength, and Hope." Billy tapped my shoulder to turn and face him and said, "I belong to AA, yet I feel more comfortable in the meetings devoted to addicts. I have a local meeting list if you want." We walked to his room, where he produced a tattered meeting list for the Berkeley area. Saying thanks and a good night in the friendly way of the recovering community (who believe a hug a day keeps the urge to drink away), I joked that I would be extra conscious of not thudding around over his head. "I'm not worried," he responds. "We're going to be friends."

In the second month of my being at school, Mom paid a visit. She slept in the extra bed in my room; I had pushed them together as one large for both studying chaise lounge style and to make room for my morning stretches. I wanted her to go with me to Tiburon and scope out the Attitudinal Healing Center. I could sense Mom would choose other lodgings on her subsequent visits as the trek down the hall to the community bath and shower just wasn't suiting her.

Before Mom's visit, an odd thing happened to confirm I was in the right place for me at the right time. Driving across the desert and up the coast highway listening to Carolyn Myss tapes, I had been wrestling with my thoughts on channeled material. I had no trouble with the Course in Miracles. Its truth rang deep in my soul. Now, if I understood Carolyn's thoughts, most of us can tap into our inner core of Beingness and allow source wisdom to flow through us. Deep meditators report greater agility in gaining access to Higher Wisdom. My beginning forays into meditation had offered me glimpses into how that worked.

Before TROT's move to Woodland Road home, I had a precognitive dream of a trail ride that would occur later on the same day with Gwen, one of TROT's most severely paraplegic riders, aboard the pony Sis. On the actual ride, our group of three mounted riders, each accompanied by a full treatment team of volunteers - two side walkers and a horse handler, arrived at a spot on the trail identical to the spot where (in my dream) a roaring three-wheeler appeared.

Arriving at that spot, I called for a full halt with focused attention and deep breathing for all. Minutes later a three-wheeler roared around the bend and past us, throwing dirt as it skidded to avoid our group. All of us held steady. Bless Sis, the lead mare, and her pony bright mind, standing firm at the head of the group as we talked and settled ourselves. The other two horses adopted the "It's okay" attitude from Sis.

Now in Oakland, a group of my classmates carpooled to Orinda High School on the other side of our Oakland Mountain to hear EMMANUEL, a channeled entity to be introduced by Ram Dass. I joined them. Keeping my doubt to myself, I wrote on the 3 x 5 card handed out for demonstration purposes my personal question. I asked for guidance on believing in this capacity we might develop in ourselves. Was it like a muscle and if practiced and acted upon, keeping to the code of doing no harm, might I clarify my mission? I signed the card BKR (initials for my birth name, Barbara Kathleen Rector—initials my dad embroidered on a pair of my overalls as I became a toddler). At the point in the program where the small unassuming man who voiced EMMANUEL was ready for questions, his two helpers brought out the basket of cards.

He reached in and read first the question from BKR. After reading my question aloud, EMMANUEL says, "Indeed, Barbara, all of us are capable of developing access to Source Wisdom. You must practice. Take action only as your heart and your head and your gut line up in agreement." And line up they did, as a thrill bump feeling ran up my spine, neck, and arms. So much for my doubt as to the veracity of channeled material. One of the nuns remarked that it is the practice of her convent to ask and receive the same answer three times in both meditation, prayer and reverie.

Mom arrived and I settled her into my dorm room. She shadowed my classes for the day. Neither of us much cared for the cafeteria food, so she suggested we go to Target and buy a mini-fridge and coffee maker, so I could do cereal and coffee at my desk each morning. This gave me time for an early morning walk in the redwoods above the school. The woods were fragrant with the musk of earthiness of Tamarisk trees, from which I returned refreshed and creatively energized - ready for a full day and night of classes.

For much of that first fall semester, I focused on my work at the Center for Attitudinal

Healing in Tiburon. The center on the dock was a hub of activity for critically ill children and their families. I proved particularly adept at co-facilitating the family groups seeking solace and answers for how it was their child was scheduled to leave life early.

MOVING THROUGH THE VEILS

The Course in Miracles and Creation-Centered Spirituality merged with my belief system to take me further into my knowingness from my experiences on the other side. Particularly portions of my sessions with the Counsel of Lighted Beings flared forth to remind me to check my heart body mind for alignment before taking action.

Dr. Stan Grof entered my life as a teacher. He and his wife Christine offered sessions in *Holotropic Breathwork;* a process using your breath and evocative music with a trained sitter holding your psyche's kite string, you learn to enter a "non-ordinary state of consciousness. This intentionally induced experience of being both in the current concrete world of lying on a comfy mat breathing and listening while also transporting yourself elsewhere purposefully gaining shifted perspectives served to integrate my Beingingness. Journeying offered me healing integration and helpful information. The regular practice sessions built my comfort with and trust in listening and allowing Guidance. The trained 'sitter' holds your psyche's kite string to help you find your way back into your body.

Soon I was going weekly to my therapist, Theresa, in Berkeley who was trained in Holotropic Breathwork. She often held daylong groups in which we might take turns being a sitter in the morning and a breather in the afternoon. On one such daylong group, I went first as the breather. I had been frustrated by a phone conversation with my mom who was worried about my explorations in the realm of woo-woo.

Mom was off to Corregidor with her third

husband, General George Jones (who had secured the Pacific for McArthur by initiating his troops jumping out of low-flying planes in full combat gear) where they were honoring him. Mom and George were to be guests of Cory Aquino, the president of the Philippines. I settled into breathing with my eye mask on, my agreeable sitter by my side, lying comfortably on my mat in a nest of blankets and pillows.

Suddenly I am flying low over a jungle smelling of charred burning flesh. In my body in Berkeley, I am retching into the plastic bag held by my sitter. She offers a sip of water and I'm back down on my mat again flying low over a charred flesh-smelling jungle. I see a convoy of jeeps with General George in the passenger seat. Mom's luggage is wrapped in red bands and Mom is jammed into the back seat as the jeep careens along the jungle path. Up ahead I see an ambush waiting to jump the jeeps and open fire. George, George, I am frantically pounding on his back. Stop! Turn back! Ambush ahead. Restless, George tries to shake off my pounding. He tells the driver to stop. All pause. There are several in a front jeep filled with soldiers and two jeeps in the rear.

George seems to sniff the air. He tells the driver to turn around. Something is not right. As the jeeps turn and head back the waiting soldiers begin to follow them, screaming and shooting. The cavalcade makes it to a white stucco building, under the portico Mom and General are shepherded inside. Mom is ushered into a bathroom to hunker down with other women. The General starts telling soldiers and guards where to station themselves and how to keep attackers out. Eventually, more government troops arrive and again take Mom and General in a jeep in a different direction. They head for an ancient airstrip where an old-fashioned twin-engine plane has landed. The jeep goes directly to the stairs being let down. Mom and George help each other up. Mom's luggage is thrown with General's ancient leather duffle into the plane's hold. Steps go up and Mom and General are holding hands and praying.

As I struggle to wake up and return to my Berkeley mat, sitter, and Theresa, I am thinking that could not have been real. Mom would never strap her lovely luggage with those stout red tapes around her bags; it is so unsightly. I have been breathing all afternoon through both sessions and into the early evening. Theresa helps me center and come back to this three-dimensional world. My friend from the dorm says she will drive me home in my car. Her boyfriend brings her car. Before we leave Theresa and Lynn hear the tale of my journey. That was some trip! Lynn lives on my floor and agrees to keep an eye on me.

Back in the dorm, I assure Lynn I'm fine. After heating chicken soup in the lounge microwave, I sit sipping hot soup and listening to my phone messages. "Barbara, this is the State Department. Your mother and the General have been detained in an attempted coup of Corregidor and their host president, Mrs. Aquino." The message included a number to call to learn the details of their rescue, which was a work in progress. Lynn spun around and listened, fascinated as I learned that my afternoon journey might have been to an actual location along with my mom and her husband, General George Jones.

Eventually, I get through to the State Department number and after identifying myself am told that Mom and George have been successfully extracted from the jungle and after a stop on an island with a larger airport will be put on a flight to L.A. and then on up to San Francisco. They are scheduled to arrive in San Francisco around 1 am. They will call to confirm once the plane has left L.A. with them on it so I might use the LA to SF flight time to drive over to the airport and collect them. Good grief. I tell Lynn, I'm going to sleep and set my alarm for midnight.

Practical thinking Lynn asks about where they will stay. Aha. There is a charming old hotel spa resort, The Clairemont, on the way to Berkeley from our dorm. I call and say that my parents are coming in unexpectedly and required a room. I give them my credit card (I have my own). It will be about two in the morning by the time I collect them at SF airport. I settle in to breathe and pray and am soon fast asleep.

The phone awakens me at 11:45 pm. The State Department tells me that Mom and George have been successfully loaded onto the night shuttle and I affirm I will collect them. After a long slow hot shower, I dress. There is little to no traffic for the quick trip from my dorm in Oakland to the airport just across the Bay Bridge. This is in the days before tight airport security and I am waiting at their gate.

They are ecstatic to see me. Mom is full of their amazing adventure and praises George's talent for organization and leadership. I am busy hugging them both, grateful for their safety, and gently herding them to baggage claim. I have said nothing about my breath work journey when Mom's bags arrive, wrapped in bright red straps, just as I'd seen in my session.

"I think I know what's been happening," I say. We make our way to my Trolley Trooper and load the bags. The General wants the back seat so he can stretch out his long legs. "Yeah, you were pretty cramped in that jeep ride through the jungle where you were almost ambushed," I say. "I have reservations at that charming Inn on the edge of Berkeley." And as I drive, I tell them what has happened to them on their adventure. Both are silent and intent.

George says, "So it was you alerting me that something wasn't right up ahead." George admits to having felt great unease, with a harsh pressure on his back.

"That was me pounding on you to get your attention." I remind Mom of Bob and milepost 89 and the elk on his windshield. We get to the Inn and settle them into their room. As George takes a shower, Mom and I cuddle on the king-size bed. She wants to know more about how it was I journeyed. I explain Holotropic Breathwork. No drugs, simply breathing to evocative music with an eyeshade over your eyes. I say to Mom, "Let me try something out on you".

With Mom's agreement, I tell her how one of my first sessions made a lot of sense to me and helped explain my feeling all my life about being her caretaker. In this journey, I become aware I am in her womb. She is on a bus in the very back seat, riding up and down the main line. Not getting off, just riding back and forth in the harsh sun of a dusty western town—Temple, Texas. I am aware that she has just learned she is pregnant. She is terrified; she doesn't know if she can do this Mom thing. She is due home to tell Dad and share what ought to be wonderful news. And for Mom, it isn't. She is just not feeling prepared.

Mom is tearful as I tell her this story. She is full of angst, explaining that it is indeed a true story. That is what happened. "You were but a little fertilized egg. How could you be aware? Conscious in my womb? How is that possible?" I explain that I am not seeking validation. My point was that the story helped me.

While Mom goes to shower, I'm dozing on the bed. George invites me to stay. It's a huge bed. He just wants a little nap until breakfast. Mom comes out to lie down with us. I shift so she is next to George. We three sleep until late morning and then have an amazing breakfast. I take them to school with me and then over to the Attitudinal Healing Center. They both fit right in and tell me they feel very much at home.

Dr. Jerry (Jampolsky) tells me they are probably somewhat in shock and to keep them close. I invite them to hike the redwoods with me the next day and do a beach picnic and think about flying home the following day. They do as I suggest.

In my absence TROT was going full speed into developing hippotherapy a treatment by physical therapists, occupational therapists, and speech and language therapists trained to be clinical specialists in Hippotherapy. HPOT works with the movement horses produce to strengthen trunk and core muscles, and increase righting proprioception sense while offering the student a fun activity doing something many of their peers do not do.

More about this and other specialty domains of medical treatment with the help of horses is included in the white paper commissioned by Watermark Properties. It is shared by request to Barbara. See addendum. Barbarakrector42@gmail.com

Over Christmas break, Jeremey Taylor challenged our class to practice lucid dreaming. On New Year's Eve, we were to make an intention to show up as a class on the steps of the Acropolis in Greece. We were to greet each other, wish Peace in the New Year, hug and depart. I have never been to Greece and was excited by this challenge. Thrilled too at the possibility of at least touching in with Billy over the extended school vacation, I was surprised at what happened.

My memory says we as a class of eight 'dreamers' made it to the Acropolis steps and greeted each other. At the point of hugging Billy, we had somehow saved each for last; we both wink out of our collective lucid dream and flash into the tobacco fields of North Carolina. There I am walking along the rows with him as he discusses with his foreman the crop and its needs.

Just as I am wondering if Billy knows I am there with him, he says, "Barbara, let's get you out of this heat and onto the shaded porch for some of Hattie's sweet tea". He takes my hand; I can feel him feeling me. Billy guides me over to an ancient mud-spattered jeep and helps me into the passenger side. "Goddess what a southern gentleman", I am thinking.

Billy takes me to his white pillared generous wrap-around porch home where his Mom and sisters live. On the front porch, we sit in rockers under the ceiling fans as Hattie brings out a tray of tea and cookies. I am as real to Hattie as she is to me. Astonished, she is my Maudie, the lady housekeeper who cared for me and Walt and Susan in our Charleston, West Virginia youth. So much a part of our family, Maudie moved to Cleveland with us. Hattie could be Maudie's twin sister.

Billy's Mom and her two Bueaviers, large dogs that resemble mini bears appear on the porch for their morning walk; she does not see me. The Beauv who resembles my own Sugar Bear (now actually sleeping at foot of my bed in the Morningstar Casita where I lived) does see me. Sissy is sniffing and elbowing me for an ear rub. I comply.

Billy's Mom is exclaiming over Sissy's weird head movements towards the chair where I am sitting and scratching her ears. Both Billy and Hattie smile and wink at me. I am whisked back to my Casita in Tucson, AZ. Good Grief! Did that happen? I don't even know how to call Billy. Our friendship had yet to progress to sharing contact information.

Back at school in mid-January, I am eager to bump into Billy. No luck until the first morning of Dream Class. We assemble and are quizzed by Jeremey as to our success. Our journals are read and shared with the class. We all agreed we had seen each other on the steps of the Acropolis. One of the Nuns said that as Billy and Barbara hugged they disappeared together. Did you stay together, she wants to know.

Billy nods. YES, we dropped back into my tobacco fields and I took her to my front porch for tea. Our Hattie could see her, but not my Mom. One of Mom's dogs knew her. Sissy had a good ear rub. The whole class turns to me.

YES, the experience was astonishing. Billy's Mom's dog Sissy is so very similar to my own Sugar Bear. They could be sisters. And Hattie might as well be a twin to our beloved Maudie. Truly, it was a singular experience. I don't think Billy's foreman saw me. No, he never mentioned anything to me. And YES, Hattie did see you as did Sissy.

Jeremey discusses the collective soul connection of all of us in the dream group. It was his first successful whole class of students making the date and hugging each other. He wanted Billy and me to probe further as to what our psychic heart connection might be. It is obvious to the class that Billy and I have an easy rapport and so very much in common. What exactly remains is a mystery.

With the spring semester underway, Billy's class is making graduation plans. I know I will miss him terribly. We did make a date to work on a subsequent dream that we both recorded and brought to class. We dreamed a very similar dream the same night before class. Billy is dressed in a tux and driving a John Deer tractor. I show up next to him riding my chestnut mare Rama. We are tricked out in our Prix St. Georges competition show clothes, top hat, and double bridle. White breeches, yellow vest, and black tailcoat with snowy white stock.

The dream segues into the two of us dancing the waltz in dress dinner clothes, swirling amongst a crowded floor of waltzing partners. We are easy, graceful, and rhythmic as we flow together. Jeremy quickly determines that no, we have not further investigated our apparent psychic heart connection. He affirms the dream is suggesting unfinished business of interpersonal and even transpersonal nature demanding answers. When asked how we felt on awakening from our collective dream, we both answered "GREAT".

After class, Billy suggests we eat dinner together in the cafeteria that night and explore this soul affinity. OK Sure. In the cafeteria we found a table to spread out our journals and begin to look at the period of Billy's first semester and my adventures six months before coming to Oakland.

We start with an extended discussion of why we came to Holy Names and what we were seeking in the way of validation for the life we were living. Billy spoke of his crossroads, engagement to Harriett, angst at his family's business (tobacco), and duties as Commissioner of Agriculture for South Carolina. He was drawn to Holy Names for the spiritual nature of the studies offering practical life applications. He was fairly solid in his recovery and was in therapy to help cure his stuttering.

"What stuttering," I say. "Well, that's the odd thing, Barbara. When I am around you I don't stutter". Billy is serious. He tells me the whole first semester he hardly said a word in class to avoid his dreaded nemesis stuttering. Yet I come along that first morning at breakfast and banter with him about our childhood merry-go-round rides on Myrtle Beach and there is no sign of stuttering.

"Ah, well now you know that I seem to have detail blindness with people," I tell Billy the story of how one of the ushers at my elaborate wedding in Cleveland said to me how adorable he found my friend Wendy. It was too bad about her wandering fish eye. I regard him, astonished. Later seeing Wendy, I am peering intently at her, this high school best friend in our little gang of best friends (Mary, Harriett, and Wendy). Wendy has dry humor. She stares back at me and says, "Who told you about my eye deal?"

The cafeteria folks are closing and want to lock up for the night. Billy and I gather our stuff and begin to walk back to our dorm. He suggests we detour to stand in the Nun's garden and view the city lights. Standing shoulder to shoulder as we did most Wednesday class nights during the break, Billy asks, "Was Wendy aware you never noticed her wandering eye up until then?"

"YES, we talked later about it and shared it with Harriett and Mary. They confirmed that I just never appear to notice the cracks and holes in people."

Billy suggests I walk to his room and come in to see a picture he has brought from home. It is the Myrtle Beach merry-go-round. I am delighted. He says, "Say listen, you want to go to the movies? **Field of Dreams** has just opened at the Oakland Fox."

"I love movies! When?"

"Now", he says.

"Now! It's 10:30 pm.", I exclaim.

"Well, we'll make the 11 pm showing if we go now. Leave your stuff here and come. You won't need your purse."

So off we go. Billy drives a gold Mercedes sports car. We're at the Oakland Fox Theatre in a flash. For parking, he takes a curb spot and hangs an Official's badge from the rearview mirror. Billy is also a South Carolina State Constable.

The evening is surreal. As he buys the tickets I head for the women's room up ornate red velvet-covered stairs with gilded gold handrails. I head down the stairs as he's buying popcorn. He sees me coming and advances up the stairs to give me his arm. Yours is the un-buttered he tells me.

Without words, we head down the almost empty darkened theatre to take seats mid-way on the aisle. My spot and also his; the movie begins and it is another time warp. I sense feel I am in the movie and Billy is with me. We are leaning companionably into each other. Or is it mutual support?

The movie concludes and we both simply sit. Finally, Billy says to me "Believe" and he stands offering me his arm. We make our way back to his car lost in our post-movie reveries. Back at the dorm, we discover we are locked out. Neither of us being night owls, we had missed the curfew midnight rule. It is now 2 am. Billy uses the wall phone to call the dorm prefect, a crusty nun who is not pleased with being roused from her precious sleep.

Billy walks me to his room to collect my books and then gallantly walks me up the stairs to my room where we exchange hugs. Thank you, I say. "Yes, he says I'm glad we did it and we saw the movie together. It helps confirm our dream sharing".

The following day we are the talk of the school. Our late-night lockout is being discussed amongst dorm residents. Jeremey is curious in class. Did our outing help us to retrieve further information on our apparent soul connection? I volunteer how uncharacteristically I behaved. Going out with no purse, no identification. The whole adventure simply felt 'right'. For me it felt like being in a movie within a movie; one that I had been through before.

Billy said he agreed about the feeling of repeating an already lived experience. He said it was odd how he knew I took unbuttered popcorn and *"where we generally liked to sit in movie theatres".* Jeremey took careful note of our language and suggested we intensify our practice of logging our dreams. He wondered if we were familiar with the concept of simultaneous alternative realities.

Jeremey's further probing uncovered that we were both in therapy with a Berkley professional who specialized in psychotherapy with Holotropic breath work. This was new information to us. Leaving class together, I asked Billy if his counselor was named Theresa. Yes, he confirmed; she used to be an OBGYN. Ah ha....we share the same therapist I told him.

Plans for the Spring Graduation of Billy's class were in full sway. The nuns had organized dance classes in the large hall of the dorm. A hired professional put us through the swing steps of current styles including the box steps of the waltz and the step slide together of the fox trot. I loved the classes and rather wished that Billy was participating. I would catch him grinning at our group efforts as he whizzed through the hall to the mail desk.

One late afternoon early dusky evening in May there was an all-school rehearsal of the graduation processional. As the nuns organized our groups and attempted to impose discipline on our designated lineup, spontaneous dancing broke out. Suddenly the fragrant garden was alive with laughter and square dancing do si dos. Billy caught me up in his strong arms and whirled me around off the ground. It felt to me like we had done that same swirling turn forever; even the slide down his broad chest to stabilize my feet on the ground. He held me there and time-shifted. We meshed. Then he abruptly disappeared.

The young nun from our dream class commented that the whole of last year, Billy had been remote, keeping to himself; no one had been able to draw him out or learn much about him. Then I come along and he is seen out and about more engaging with our class and activities. I shrug and admit that I find him an easy fascinating friend. Especially captivating are our odd synchronistic experiences of dream overlays.

Several nights later there was a special Chapel celebration of Via Creativa. The conclusion of this moving ceremony honoring the creative spirit alive in us was a period of silence. Slowly we became aware of Ravelle's building throbbing music of Bolero. A capped and hooded figure appeared floating amongst our benches swirling to the rhythmic intensity of this evocative piece. I sense a feeling of Billy. The dancer's identity was never revealed and yet I knew "since feeling" Billy.

The following week after dream class, I tell Billy I have invited Theresa and her husband to the graduation dinner and dance. Well, I also invited her and Tommy he tells me. We'll need to arrange to share a table. You can save me a dance. I've been watching your lessons. My favorite is Southern Swing. What is that? It doesn't sound familiar. Billy tells me it's a wild active form of jitter-bug. Lots of swinging and twirling; he belongs to a club back home. It's where and how he met Harriett, his fiancée.

I walk away reminding myself I don't poach on another's territory. I recognize I am halfway in love with the idea of Billy. I don't know him.

The night of the dance I am feeling pretty in a new swirl skirt with a glittery top that accents my slender waist and trim, athletic body. I walk every day and manage to ride horseback two evenings a week and both days of the weekends. I school a friend's second-level dressage mare Spirit at a local private barn in the Oakland hills. More about this story of Spirit and her amazing owner, the globally known astrologist Patricia Sun will be shared in book two.

Theresa and I greet each other and head for a table where Billy has organized a reserved sign placed. There are several members of our dream class seated as we arrive. Billy comes in and starts up a conversation with Tommy. Our dinner conversation is easy and free much like that breakfast meeting on my first day of graduate school. This time rather than across the table, Billy has seated us next to each other side by side with Theresa on his right side and Tommy on my left.

Once the speeches and prayers conclude, the tables are cleared and pushed back to make room for the dance floor. Billy takes my hand as the music starts up and suggests we go see how the dance lessons worked. He means the whole table; all eight of us circle dancing to the sweet rhythm of Here We Go Again. Our group dance encouraged the others who soon crowd onto the floor.

The second song is live rock and roll. I am remembering Barbara Ann. Billy takes my hand to partner and leads me into a rhythmic southern swing dance. Astounding; it is as if we have danced and danced together for centuries. As the beat increases, he soon has me swinging up over his shoulder and flying through the air.

Couples stop to circle our antics and cheer us on. Billy can Dance!

Miraculously my body behaves as if I have studied and partnered with him for the whole of our lives. It is glorious. When the music segues into a slow soothing cheek-to-cheek, Billy pulls me close, the lights dim and I surrender to the feelings of completeness. We pretty much dance the whole night away. Occasionally Billy does the polite gentlemanly thing and shares the wealth of his talent with our dream group of nuns. He always says he will be back to collect me. He is true to his word and cuts in on others partnering with me. He returns to pull me in close.

Tommy shares a dance with me as Billy and Theresa do a lively step hop. Once the last dance begins, Billy seeks me out to pull me in chest close and we seem to simply sway and be in the moment. I remember his final squeeze and then the gut wrench as he set me apart from him. Both of his hands slid down my arms and holding my hands firmly he peered intently down into my eyes. "I will always ALWAYS remember you. I will always take your call. You have my number. Please use it."

My eyes blurred with tears as Billy abruptly disappears. He left. I am filled with empty sadness and full-hearted gladness at having had this experience with Billy. Theresa and Tommy appear at my side offering comfort. They want to walk with me to the dorm and see my room and how it is exactly above Billy's.

Together we walk up the dorm stairwell; the site of the late evening harmonica concerts when Billy could not sleep. Together with the other hall mates, we would sit in our PJs above Billy who sat on the steps a floor below us, his feet stretched out on a bottom stair, back to the wall, serenading us with haunting southern hymns.

The three of us reach my door and there propped against it is a book. No note, no sign of who left it there for me to discover. On the way up to my third floor, I showed them Billy's former door. We all knew he had left the building. He had a late-night red eye to the east coast and home. It is a curious thing about the book.

I've never learned who left it for me. I have my suspicions.

The Kiss of the Snow Queen by Hans Christian Anderson and *Man's Redemption by Woman* by Wolfgang Lederer. Sometimes I decode the mystery as me the loyal friend who rescues the Prince (Billy) from his isolated castle prison, a slave to the Snow Queen. Billy's addictive drug of choice was snow (cocaine). His nemeses had been stuttering. A thing of the past as our dancing dinner evening had demonstrated.

I will never forget my friend Billy.

TRAVELING

Now for the promised story of my friend Nancy and my returning home from England and our first International Riding for the Disabled Conference (1978). We left off at Dame Edith's castle to make our way to London Heathrow airport where we are caught up in the craziness of the world's poorest signage in a giant public terminal.

During the check-in process, Nancy and I become separated. I am pressured into following the airline person directing us to a shuttle bus that takes us out on the tarmac to a parked 747. I am being told that my friend has her ticket and is likely already in her seat. We are amongst the last group of passengers to be boarded.

The shuttle bus parks at the steps leading up to the plane's doorway. Two stories up for the front door and another story above that, I climb up praying to find Nancy. I see ahead to our seats and she is not there. I demand an attendant seek her out and page her. No Nancy. I refuse to take my seat. I return to the front door as they are beginning to take the steps away. I throw out my carry bag and grab for the rail, two stories up I leap across the growing chasm as the stairs are being driven away from the plane.

A siren shrieks as the airport Bobbies drive up to the moving stairs. They meet me at the bottom to tell me I am under arrest. "If you can arrest me, you can find my friend, Nancy," I explain how we were separated during check-in; and my persistent questioning of her whereabouts. I look up pointing to the glass lounge where we had been processed and there pressed against the glass is my horrified and delighted friend Nancy. She has seen my daring leap.

Rather than arrest, we are turned over to the airline personnel who promptly book us on the next morning's flight to New York LaGuardia. They handle the rebooking on connecting flights now being missed to get us to Tucson. We are courtesy guests of the airlines at a lovely hotel, with robes, room service, and toiletries. Calling our husbands about not coming home until a day later, we learn that our scheduled flight into LaGuardia had to be rerouted due to crowding on the runways protecting the Pope's visit to New York.

Such travel adventures with Nancy were to be repeated two more times. Our 1983 trip to Milan Italy for the International Riding for the Disabled Conference and then again in 1993 another adventure RDI Conference to Auckland New Zealand where we were both invited speakers. Nancy on her recently published research on childhood spasticity and Hippotherapy and me with my work developing Equine Facilitated Psychotherapy for adolescents in residential treatment with dual diagnoses of substance abuse and mental health issues.

In Auckland, I meet again with Dr. Kluwer who invites me to co-chair with him a gathering of mental health delegates and riding instructors to discuss some of the interesting findings we are discovering on how horses prompt patients into writing their treatment plans. Dr. Kluwer's mentorship of me in EFP is recounted in the Watermark Retirement Communities commissioned white paper. (July 2015) available upon request to Barbara@adventuresinawareness.net

We developed the practice of having the adolescents write up a training plan for their horse, mutually chosen, that they worked with regularly. Unaware of the similarities between their horse and their issues, actual mirrors of behavior, these patients designed their treatment plan. They told us what would work for them. We shared these plans in staffing sessions to weave the equine-facilitated psychotherapy throughout their treatment protocols.

The story of our 1983 trip to Milan Italy evokes the emergency Master Card use as well as illustrates Ram's inherent love of the mother of his children – me. On the final day of the conference when we are scheduled to visit the Italian Cavalry Quarters, I am sitting in the hotel lobby waiting for Nancy and reading. When I read, I disappear into the book. I have missed planes by reading through the gate announcements.

Nance appears and I reach down under my chair to grab my purse and it is not there. Gone; it was lifted during the unawareness of my surroundings while reading. Holy Cat Fish! I am now missing my passport, my airline ticket home, my jewelry, my spare teeth (front partial plate residual damage from my NDE) all my money, my driver's license, and my credit card. It is late summer of our June 22, 1983 divorce degree and Ram has insisted I keep the Master card in my name of Barbara Kathleen Rector-Morken.

After our London adventure, we two friends had already agreed to never leave our 'wingman', thus Nancy tells the Conference director we will not be on the bus. We have other more urgent business. Barbara's purse has been stolen. The hotel calls the police who have me fill out a report. They invite us to the nearby police station, not in the best area of central Milan. The women's bathroom was a tiled pee hole that you squatted over. UGH.

The police helped us set up a lost passport report, directed us to the US Embassy for help in obtaining another, gave us directions to a photographer for a suitable passport photo, and suggested we needed to call home to notify our families. Also, a call to the airline canceling our seats on the next day's flight home; would need approximately five to seven days for passport replacement. Double UGH. And I needed money to rebook and buy whole new airline tickets for us both. International in those days required the purchase of a new ticket for both of us. Later Nancy was reimbursed (she still had her ticket) and I was able to send that money on to Ram.

YES, I called home to Ram and requested a

loan be wired to our hotel. At the end of our very long day, waiting at our hotel through Western Union was $5,000 to purchase two one-way tickets from Milan to Tucson, five days on Lake Como where we two adventured while awaiting the arrival of my passport, our meals, and our lodgings. Nancy is the very best travel companion in the world. She and her trusty guidebook are funds of information on where to go, what to do, and where to stay economically.

Two interesting items about our extended Italy stay. At the US Embassy, we take the elevator to the top floor as directed in the lobby. The elevator door opens and we are confronted by a line of armed military rifles at the ready. Nancy slams the close door button. The two of us are like what the heck? I am affirming I saw Reagan's picture behind the soldiers. We push the open door button and this time the soldiers are standing at attention rifles on their shoulders.

Their leader steps forward to say, "Yes this is the US Embassy. You are in the right place. He tells us there is a situation brewing and is sorry to have scared us."

Standing at the lost passport window, teasing out the process of replacing my passport, I am lost on the name of the county in Texas where I was born. Turning my head aside, I am staring at an AA meeting list. There is one being held in a nearby coffee shop later that afternoon. Nancy peers over and affirms that we will both go. We do; it helped.

Touring and exploring Lake Como for the next several days, we are out of touch with the world's happenings. Our small pension notifies us that the Embassy called. It had my passport and our airline tickets ready for the next day. At the Milan airport, once checked in and watching the news on the waiting room TV, we discover that by missing our previously booked flight, the one we were scheduled to be on had my purse not been stolen……we missed being hijacked and held on the tarmac of Rome airport for over a week….we were not amongst those passengers we were seeing on TV still being held hostage on the plane sitting in Rome.

Just before Christmas break at Holy Names, as we waited for our grade postings, I had a note in my mailbox to please go visit the Academic Dean. This lovely nun gets right to her point. Your grades are excellent. How is it you are not enrolled to obtain an advanced degree? I explain how poorly I test. My undergraduate grade point would have also been excellent, had I not failed Philosophy 101 Introduction five times at three major Universities. YES, I noticed that on your transcript.

What was the problem? Well, I misunderstood the class process. It wasn't until my godfather, Dean of Liberal Arts, Fran Roy at U of A talked to me. He had read my tests at U of A and discovered that I was giving my thoughts on the readings. This was a NO-NO. The professors were looking for my comments on their lectures and thoughts. Humm, says lovely Holy Names Dean. I suspected. I want to propose you consider completing your studies in Psychology – MA in Spiritual Psychology. We will admit you on academic probation and depending on your work during the Spring semester, we would take you on for degree completion that Fall and next Spring.

Wow, I am excited! Back in Tucson, I consult with TROT and Nancy. They are doing well; Nancy counsels me to go for it. I discovered my work-study would be renewed. Dr. Jampolsky offered me an intake counselor-paying job over the summer. A classmate had room to share (sublet) in an Oakland apartment overlooking downtown Lake Merritt. I might use the extra time to get a good start on my thesis.

Mom was very encouraging. Neither of us doubted that my upcoming spring semester would be anything but graduate school standard. Working and living in downtown Oakland, gave me a feeling of reverse discrimination. In the apartment basement laundry room, in the elevators, and out and about on the streets and the walking area around Lake Merritt, it begins to dawn on me that I am practically a lone white person amongst all sorts of other color backgrounds and cultures.

Towards the end of that summer, Dr. Jampolsky suggests I make contact with a therapeutic riding center south of San Francisco in Woodside. The National Center for Equine Facilitated Therapy (NCEFT) may be willing to help some of our terminal clients to have an experience of riding horses safely. It might also be suitable for some of the Center's Adults with Homebound Disabilities, a fascinating group I had been facilitating weekly during the summer.

SYNCHRONICITIES

Jerry wanted me to go check it out and speak to the current director and therapist about possibilities. I asked Nancy if she had ever heard of National Center for Equine Facilitated Therapy (NCEFT) and she discovered that they also belonged to NARHA – now PATH International. The Denver office gave me the name of the NCEFT physical therapist that I called to make a visiting talk possibilities appointment.

Arriving at the Center on the appointed day, I am walking down the wooden stairs from the parking lot to see a woman on her knees with her backside to me and her head in an open

PORTALS TO MULTIDIMENSIONALITY

door that I took to be the office. She is wearing a skirt, nylons, and heeled pumps. I bend down to see if she needs help. We are both on our knees on the wooden landing. She looks at me and says can you reach this cable connection?

I lean past her stretched arm to peer behind a huge bank of electronic equipment to see her holding a huge connector cable. She is unable to reach the socket. Let me try. I take the cable and press around her to push it into the outlet. I am short and this older woman is even shorter. She face-to-face resembles my paternal grandmother, Budge.

She is Phoebe Cooke, owner, operator, President of the Board, and founder of NCEFT. I tell her I am from Dr. Jampolsky Attitudinal Healing Center here to visit with Audrey, her Center's physical therapist. Well, Audrey had to go home to her sick child and won't be able to show me around. Phoebe will tour me and explore possibilities. I am there for over four hours and depart with a job offer for the next winter. Phoebe wanted me to act as her center manager and live in her barn apartment. I agreed to consider the proposal and made a date to return to visit with Audrey about the center's clients and their needs.

While Dr. Jampolsky also wanted me to work for him, he did understand that the pull of the horses and my heart's passion for helping share horses with others in need prevailed. Phoebe recognizing my feelings of being pulled threw into her offer that I might bring my dog Sugar to live with me in the apartment over her barn. I might also ride her vaulting horses through the wooded trails behind the Woodside village homes to work.

YES, I did miss Billy being at school and YES I was so flat-out busy that there wasn't much time for feelings of lingering grief. By this time I had met Patricia Sun, the globally known Astrologer who led the tourist group to Chernople in Russia and was there during the nuclear reactor explosion. They were held over for decontamination treatment for several extra weeks.

Back in my dorm room at Holy Names in Oakland, I am going four to five days a week to a private barn nestled in the hills where Patricia boarded her precious second-level mare Spirit. Our meeting had been synchronous. Early fall of my second year, I visited several barns in the Oakland hills asking for someone who might need a schooling rider for their horse. I was seasoned at the second and third levels.

At about the third barn, a pleasant woman called the barn where Patricia's horse boarded and asked the owner if Spirit still needed a schooling rider. Yes, come right on over as Patricia had yet to leave town on her upcoming trip. I arrived at the barn and met the owner who also operated a tack store out of her office. She helped me speak to Patricia on the phone. We made a date to meet the following Wednesday when she had a lesson with her dressage coach who flew in from Seattle monthly. Patricia and her trainer would interview me and determine if I might help with Spirit.

As I am leaving, I ask the owner if I might meet Spirit. Well, let's see if she agrees to that plan. As we exit the office I am looking over some 40 horses in shaded individual paddocks under the large earthy tamarack trees. One extraordinary chestnut mare lifts her head to nicker at me. The barn owner affirms that is Spirit. We walk over to say hello. Spirit comes up the hill – her paddock is generously large and spacious, she approaches the fence and softly blows on my extended hand. Ah Ha, I have this lovely feeling of meeting a new and special friend.

MOM'S GHOST

GAMMY ACTIVE, VOCAL, AND DIRECTIVE AT MORNINGSTAR

Two weeks ago I had an internal adventure call and followed guidance to drive up the back road of Bonanza, the road off Fort Lowell that travels south towards the northern boundary of our old family pony paddock at MorningStar. My Mom, Kathleen Louise Spriggs Wager Rector Dayton Jones Wycoff, (Yes, two dads and four husbands – all remarkable men) had built her 'dream' home on the property she set aside after selling the original main home to finance the General's (Jones) final days with Lou Gehrig's at LaPosada in Green Valley.

Kelly, Barbara and her man Higgins, 2022.

My new man, Higgins, a one-year-old (adopted less than three months ago from the Humane Society) is supposed to be a mixture of Min-Pin/Chihuahua, accompanying me. We're in the bonding go everywhere together phase which given his 'sweet boy' personality is likely to last a lifetime. Vanilla II's trusted 2001 Subaru Forrester had engaged her low gear four wheels chugging over deep gravel as I searched for a fence line that wasn't there. I felt/sensed I was in my Dad's original vegetable garden north of the original MorningStar and pulled to a stop. I got out of my car to look westward down into my Mom's backyard of the pony paddock.

There was a youthful man with white hair standing on the back porch, hands on hips staring up the hill at me. "Hi", I wave. "I used to live here".

He responds with, "In this house or the big one?"

"Both", I shout back.

"Are you a Rector?"

"Yes, I am"

'You must be Barbara, the matriarch". He steps off the porch and starts up the hill toward me.

I'm given pause. No one has ever called me Matriarch. Yet; I reflect on its truth. I am the remaining Rector Matriarch. "Yes, I am Barbara".

The white-haired man starts walking up the steep hill through what has become a lush fruit tree garden. Mom must love what he's done to the grounds. They are Awesome. "I want to talk with you. I'm researching your Mom. She was an astonishing woman. She contributed so much culturally to our presidio. A true Grand Dame of Tucson, she founded the Opera, established the Pioneers Society as part of the U of A campus, and brought Symphony and Ballet into sustainable operations. Did she not like theatre?"

I am stunned and have lost my voice. He's raving in love with my Mom and is speaking as if they are in a relationship. "Do you have some time? Come meet the wife. Bring your dog. Just leave the car. I'll help you get it out when you go."

As he nears me, I see he's a sandal Bermuda shorts-wearing youngish man about Manfred's age (early fifties son-in-law) sun weathered through and through with twinkling blue eyes. "Hi, I'm Steve. Steven Sheldon, former owner of Tanque Verde Green House. My wife Sue and I are both now retired. We were so lucky and happy to be able to acquire this house out of bank foreclosure 16 months ago".

We shake hands. I feel the tingly warmth of loving familiarity. In some odd sense, we've known each other before and not yet met face-to-face in this plane of existence. This sparking alive pulsing is known to me from my first encounter on the interior stair steps of Campbell Ave. Bank in 1973 first meeting Bazy in the company of my best friend, Nancy. The three of us would go on to cofound Therapeutic Riding of Tucson, Inc.

Back in the MorningStar pony paddock, I looked around the exterior of the old home in amazement. It appeared to be the house it always wanted to be rather than the hilltop Grecian temple Mom erected. Sue came to the back door and invited us to enter. She's lovely with equally twinkly blue eyes and youthful sparkle energy attached to two adorable female Yorki minis. They are immediately falling all over my man Higgins. I keep him leashed and I hope somewhat protected.

Walking into the main room from the back,

the spectacular vista of the city-wide basin is in your face. The already generous room has been opened up and enlarged. Front window shutters were removed and no walls at all from the living room fireplace east to the edge of the breakfast room beyond the kitchen. Whew. "Wow, this is simply Stunning! Mom would love what you've done."

"Well, yes and no", says Sue. "She keeps us informed on her feelings. We all hear her. Especially when she's yelling at what seems to be two different Bills".

Astonished I look at her with raised eyebrows and my 'are you kidding me' expression. My belly button Dad Bill Rector and 4th acquired step-dad Bill Wycoff must be the 'said' Bills. "Are you kidding me?" I exclaim.

"Only the men, Steven, and my son see her. But we all hear her", declared Sue.

Steven is nodding his head affirmatively. "We're both rather spiritual and this sort of thing is not new to us. Kathleen is truly active in our days working with us to rehabilitate the home. It had fallen into rack and ruin as the buyers from her estate simply got in over the heads".

Eagerly they took me about throughout the entire house and the guest house Casita including its garage that now has a Saltillo tile floor to house the indoor sauna. Ah, my body responds lustfully to the sauna. Sitting In one is the only time I'm aware of pain-free feelings in my body. The Sheldons have easily sunk at least the original cost of the home into the remodeling improvements. The driveway is now concrete. The whole driveway and Casita apron are concrete and the deck around the overhanging porches has been expanded a foot out around the exterior - this deck eight times around made Bill Wycoff's daily mile walk.

They have saved Mom's treasured blue garden gate. They told me they are making a Park of the entire surrounding grounds. Kathleen is helping. While she didn't like the master bath changes (removed bidet) or the filling in of her pool house to make Sue's office; the collaboration on the Park is something Steven tells me he looks forward to as her ideas are voiced with their daily check-ins.

I told them Mom stories in answer to their questions; I spent over two hours. We exchanged promises to return visits and shared phone numbers and email addresses. As Sue and Steven walk me to the car, I tell them that I've always wondered how it is Mom never appeared to me. She left in April of 04. When my Dad died in 79, I had his ghost with me at intermittent intervals until a Bay area shaman helped me send him on to the Light in 1989.

I gave Steven and Sue a hug and told them both that I am so glad Mom has people who admire and appreciate her listening to her directives and following through in doing what she wants. "While she was a tremendously remarkable woman, she was an awesomely DIFFICULT mother", I exclaim.

"Oh Yes", says Sue. "We get that. Her yelling can be hurtful. I'm glad I don't see her. Steven says she looks like the picture of her Opera Board days; a very Beautiful Woman. I think he's half in love with her."

Driving away, I realize I've had one of those soul messages from God Source Energy. I'm on purpose. Move at the pace of Guidance. Call little brother Walt and let him know why it is Mom's been so quiet. I'm wondering if little sister Susan encountered her as she left unexpectedly for the lighted realms almost a year ago.

BKR/Mom/Aunt Barbara
Casita Fellowship Square
Tucson

THE STORY OF RAMA'S MAGIC

On the one-year anniversary of our Nation's historic 9/11, a group of women from Cottonwood de Tucson's InnerPath workshop gathered at AIM HIGH Equestrian Park for a daylong ADVENTURES IN AWARENESS session. This personal growth process was co-facilitated by InnerPath therapist, Rochelle Lerner of Mpls, MN, and AIA facilitators Ann Alden and Barbara Rector, both experiential educators offering AIA's form of equine facilitated experiential learning process work.

These women from all parts of the US and Europe arrived mid-week of their community-building inner journey process; all were well practiced in supporting and nurturing each other. Compassionately, they looked inward to reality check emotionally, mentally, physically, and spiritually. Under the dense umbrella formed by ancient mesquite trees surrounding AIM HIGH's small dressage arena, the AIA horses frolicked in the sprinklers.

Magic and Mystery unfolded as these horses helped us examine the relationship of our inner realm; interior psyche's feelings, thoughts, and emotions, to outwardly expressed behaviors as reflected (mirrored) by the horses and group members. After our safety agreements and centering exercise, we moved into the heart scanning - mutual choosing interactive work with the herd. Twenty minutes of mindful 'searchlight of the heart' meditation and most participants had clearly formed bonds with the horses.

After a brief safety discussion, we reviewed the basic principles of the energy field surrounding all sentient beings. First, we practiced feeling our own field, then that of other group members, and then the horses. Healthy horses have huge easily recognizable fields. Like big old trees, these are the animals with whom to practice soft eyes seeing. Good times are dusk or early dawn.

We engaged in the AIA Con Su Permiso exercise learning to invite ourselves into the field of the horse and to intentionally listen. This practice facilitates our learning more about ourselves, the horse, and others. One participant, I'll call her Lolly, was exploring Rama's energy field. She was open and receptive, consciously releasing expectations. **Lolly intended to learn from Rama as she consciously filtered her thoughts, feelings, and emotions through the lens of her heart.**

After a few moments of reverent exploration, Lolly said to Rama's safety support person, Leslie, "What is this smell of hash, marijuana on her chest?"

Leslie responded, wisely, "I don't know. We'll need to ask Barbara".

Lolly replied, "OK, and let's also ask her about the markings, those hieroglyphics on her hoof".

Leslie answered, "OK, What markings?" Leslie is seeing an ordinary horse hoof. "What do you see?" she wisely questions.

Lolly responds, "Evidence of severe trauma through water and death". Lolly's words are emphatic. "Huge high-water trauma!"

I want to interject that we were in Tucson, a desert city in southern Arizona with twice-yearly monsoon seasons. Rama, at the time, was a 23-year-old AQHA mare who came into my life as a five-year-old. Details of that story are told elsewhere. When she entered my life, she was being trained and shown second-level dressage. Bred in Oklahoma, the dealer/trainer had originally brought her to Tucson for a wealthy client's teenager.

After a box lunch under the trees, some of us went for a brief walk around the nearby lake. Leslie and Lolly are eager to question me about Rama's history. We had reached the point on the lake path looking west down the bone-dry Tanque Verde River bed we see the barn roof and corrals for TROT. Therapeutic Riding of Tucson, Inc., co-founded by myself and best friend, Nancy McGibbon, in 1974, this traditional therapeutic riding program is devoted to equine-facilitated activities and therapies for people with disabilities seeking functional improvement with the help of horses.

Lolly asked me about the smell of hash on Rama's chest. The hair on my arms and neck rose in affirmation of truth spoken alert. My hairs remained tingly and vibrating as both Lolly and Leslie report their experiences of reading Rama's field with the Con Su Permiso exercise. Others have gathered around us as our group listened to Lolly's 'read'.

My response was, "Years and years ago during her first year in Tucson, Rama was in the company of a troubled teen. Depressed and suicidal, she burned Rama's chest with a marijuana toke. When the mare's coat is show clipped or in deep summer, it appears as if her chest has been wire cut. These are really burn marks. The dealer/trainer re-possessed Rama. She was being successfully shown first and second-level dressage leased by one of his students when I entered the picture months later".

"Whew", responded the group. "You smelled that in the field!"

Lolly made a disgusted sound and waved her arm gesturing us to move on. She asked me about the severe water trauma and death she perceived pictured on Rama's left front hoof.

My whole body trembled slightly as energy ran up and down my spine. Bumps rose on my arms and neck, I felt visibly shaken. Energy pulsed through my cells. My backbone felt intense heat.

While I was away at graduate school, RAMA worked at TROT as their HIPPOTHERAPY (HPOT) horse. With her classical training, she was comfortable in side reins being ground driven by the horse professional. HPOT is the treatment of movement dysfunctions by a clinical specialist in HIPPOTHERAPY, a licensed physical, occupational, or speech and language therapist who works with the movement the horse produces to elicit positive physical changes in the client.

Back in 1993, Gigi Sweet resided at TROT in the caretaker cottage. At that time, she served as Program Head Riding Instructor and Barn Manager. One storm dark night she was awakened by restless nickers and loud stall banging. Secure behind her stemmed flood-walled yard, she was shocked to feel and see rapidly rising water covered the ground.

Enormous effort was required to push open her solid gate. Slogging through the rapids of water she pushed at the corral gates to free the

PORTALS TO MULTIDIMENSIONALITY

horses. First out from her alpha mare stall position, Rama kept up her incessant nickering as she circled the stable yard. Rama's nickers continued to collect the herd in the open yard. Gigi struggled to push open the remaining gates freeing fourteen mares and geldings,

As Gigi grabbed her mane, stout sixteen-hand RAMA took to swimming in the swirling chest-deep flood waters. Gigi clung to Rama's mane, kicking herself along the mare's side as they moved down the TROT drive and out onto Woodland Road. With the momentum of the movement, Gigi was able to roll herself aboard Rama's broad back. Rama's head was high; she continued to call the herd with her nickers. Glancing back at the endless rising water surging through the land carrying buildings, good-sized trees, and herself and the horses, Gigi saw the rest of the group fall in behind them.

As they neared high ground, Al-Marah Arabians' farm trucks beamed lights and life-affirming help. Farm apprentices and staff formed a comforting circle and the open doors of the farm trailers beckoned. The "never thought we would need emergency flood evacuation plan" had been triggered by a worried Al-Marah farm manager, David Trexler, who had been listening to late-night weather reports and flood alerts.

Wearing nothing but their wet coats of hair the herd followed Rama's trumpeting call as she hopped into the first trailer. The rest of the horses practically loaded themselves as a shivering, shaking, drenched, pajama-clad Gigi was wrapped in a horse blanket.

Later, in the shelter of the Al-Marah covered schooling ring, while the herd rolled in the deep footing, munched grass hay, and shook off the experience, one of the older mares developed stress colic. A particular favorite of Rama's, Mimi couldn't be saved.

Lolly's "read" of extreme trauma through water, and a death from her perception of hieroglyphics on Ram's left front hoof, was highly accurate. I'm tearing up, feeling humbled with deep awe and appreciation for the depth I experience in Rama. I offered a spoken prayer of gratitude for the sacred privilege of being her designated steward, her primary caretaker.

Memories continued with my tears. We returned to the rest of the group. TROT lost three acres of ground, a port a stall shed barn, and one horse that night. But for the bravery and courage of Gigi and Rama, it might have been much worse.

My awareness sharpened. My sensitivity heightened. I sensed our group shift to the realm of the sacred and a palpable attitude of reverence prevailed in the midst of our mundane chores cleaning up our sack lunches. We prepared for the afternoon's exercise of congruent message sending in the round ring. What we now call Energetic Gestalt work.

During this phase of AIA's equine-facilitated experiential process work, participants actively engage their senses with purpose and intention to examine their interior feelings as they observe the equine-facilitated gestalts in the round ring. The circle is intentionally perceived as a sacred space where the dynamics of relationship and communication are both expressed, practiced, experienced, and witnessed. The gate into the circle serves as lintel, space between one and another - reality, awareness, consciousness.

With each gestalt's completion, participants are invited to the rail to share experiences. Witnesses check out their perceptions with the phrase, "When I see you, _____I feel_____. Was or is this true for you?"

One AIA herd member, a handsome bay Arab, Dundee worked in AIA sessions for years at Chapel Rock Retreat Center for the Episcopal Dioceses in Prescott. His story as a "sighted guide" is told in the <u>Adventures In Awareness: Learning with the Help of Horses</u> (05) book by this author. Dundee went on to become a successful endurance racer, his athletic body fitted for the long haul of desert and mountain trails. He lived at the time of this story at Aim High. When not competing, he was leased to work in AIA and appeared to slip easily into his former role facilitating equine experiential learning.

Essentially round ring psychodrama, Energetic Gestalts offer poignant mini-snapshots of an individual's habitual, generally unconscious, and preconscious version of inward reality. This quantum information-rich photograph is fueled by the horse's behavior - an action that appears to not "match" the human's outward expression. There is a felt perceptual "disconnect." Our intuition tells us something is "off", not congruent.

This mirroring behavior exhibited by the horse in relation to the human (originally a psychiatric patient) inevitably matched revelations of Psyche's internal landscape. Close observation of horse and human interactions as if under a microscope, occurred in the round ring container, studied observed by myself and staff overlaid with our knowledge of patient treatment goals and enhanced by peer patient witnessing comments.

Subsequent decades have allowed the science of mirror neurons to explain this dissonant information-gathering process. Practitioners of Equine Facilitated Psychotherapy (EFP) work consciously with probing depth questions. Experiential Educators (EFL) explore the possibilities inherent in consciously expanding awareness of one's internal process.

Distinctions between boundaries of clinical counseling probing questions that are inclusive of the patient's past include full disclosure releases, permission to treat agreements, and the presence of a licensed clinician. The experiential educator's scope remains in the present time and explores future possibilities.

From my perspective, the key to unpacking gestalts is staff trained clinically in mental health principles and practices and/or experiential educators learned in process work, who are also inherently 'horsey'. I believe solid cross-training in horse psychology and physiology is essential. The horses and their behaviors hold the projections as observed and voiced by the witnesses.

For those new to the world of horses, I find it imperative they embark on a fast track of learning through weekly lessons from a classically trained Instructor, almost daily stewardship of a horse (frequently leased or co-leased due to the pricey nature of horse keeping in modern times) plus several times a week interaction on the ground or in the saddle.

It is a premise in AIA work that horses do 'read' our minds. Mind as located in every cell of our body, and defined and illustrated in the seminal book, Molecules of Emotion, by Candice Pert, Ph.D. The horse knows we feel fear. The horse feels most uncomfortable when this reading of us is incongruent - meaning we don't know we are afraid. It is this perceived unconsciousness of our internal feelings and thoughts that creates uneasy and sometimes dangerous behaviors in horses. This same mechanism influences the behaviors of people.

A highly intuitive equine facilitator such as Dundee allowed to freely express mirroring behaviors - aspects of self in the identified individual - gifts the participants with "felt" internal insights. The observing witnesses seated outside the ring simultaneously focus inward scanning their feelings while actively practicing soft eyes viewing through the perceptual lens of their hearts.

The charismatic Dundee worked individually with several different participants, clearly demonstrating the AIA mirroring principle. Dundee is a master facilitator expressing different behaviors and energetic qualities as evoked by a particular participant's clarity of intention tied to focus and congruency. The challenge becomes conscious awareness of what picture your front brain is sending. Is the energy felt inside matching the energy of the expressed behaviors?

At one point Dundee picked up the longe wand in his teeth to waggle it at a participant who appeared lethargic and without purpose. So shut down and closed off she did not know how she felt or what she wanted. Psychoanalytic theory offers the maxim that without movement (energetically) psychic blocks are stuck. Frozen and locked behind defense mechanisms, psyche is cut off from consciousness. Self is blind to internal awareness.

Comically, Dundee offered Melanie movement. "Not clear, I'll longe you", his behavior seemed to 'say'.

Melanie first laughs and then questions, "What is he doing?"

"It appears he wants to longe you", "Get Moving". "You help him move", Melanie's witness gallery was full of suggestions.

Ann, standing next to Melanie and providing safety support, suggested, "breathe, center, look inside. What do you want?"

Long pause. "I'm not used to asking myself what I want. I think I want to play".

"Don't think!" coaches Ann. "Feel".

Short pause. Emphatically, "I WANT TO PLAY!" Dundee pricked his ears and eyed Melanie.

Ann taught her how to move her body and the wand to play a game of cut the cow with Dundee. Soon all three were huffing and puffing; especially the humans who were also smiling and laughing. Dundee was snorting, blowing, and doing a short hopping trot with his tail arched high over his back executing the "Arabian, I'm cool" dance.

As our day together drew to a close, the 9/11 theme of death and letting go on many levels had expressed. My dawning recognition internally of it being time to allow treasured VARGAS his transition moved into my conscious awareness. I'm losing the battle on pain management and it is time to help him leave. He's made it abundantly clear that his Huge Heart and Indomitable Spirit are available to me and his precious soul mate, daughter Kelly. He needs freedom from a pain-wracked body, crippled with high ringbone. It is time to honor our mutual agreement to help him leave.

We discovered time for one more round ring gestalt before our completion circle. Lolly requested a Breath With interaction with Rama in the round ring. Approached in her stall, resting after lunch, Rama indicated willingness. Leslie helped Rama move around to gently warm up stiff joints and facilitate circulation flow. She agreed to remain in the ring as Rama's safety support advocate. Lolly requested me to come with her as safety support.

Jointly attuned in purpose, we entered the

gate, portal to intentional awareness. Affirming, "We are students, we are teachers what is the lesson?" Sensing the field, we slowly moved into connection with Leslie, herself standing just on the periphery of Rama's solid vibrant field.

Then in unison, we reverently stepped into Rama's space. We chanted, "You are a student, you are a teacher, what is the lesson?" I abruptly tear up and "hear feel " her saying, "It's time to help Vargas go. You must allow him freedom from pain. His Spirit remains available. He has other adventures - without a body!"

My sobs wrenched from my gut. I turned to Leslie and Lolly. Both are openly crying. Nodding affirmatively, they have 'heard and felt' this message. I turned to the witnesses and verbalized the message of release. "It is time to let VARGAS go."

At our collective acknowledgment, Rama reached out with her neck and with her large head scooped Lolly into her chest. Similar to the movement mares make to draw foals into close protection. In response to a witness query, "Rama is mothering Lolly", Ann said from the sidelines.

In the next moment, the Extraordinary happened. Forty-five years of being with horses and I've never seen or heard this behavior. Rama arched her neck, like the swan of the water rescue story, so far up I feared she might come off the ground with her front feet. Her large head moved up and down repeatedly as she coughed up an eerie sustained human cry. Tears flowed freely from both her eyes dashing onto Leslie's hands. The sounds and up-and-down head movements continued with the tears.

Time stopped. Silence. Stillness.

Dazed, our group moved into a circle to hug each other and Rama. Slowly we made our way to the fence. Rama accompanied us. There was deep awestruck silence. I glanced at Ann. Her mouth and eyes appeared equally wide.

"What was that?" someone said.

"Some 40 years with horses and I've never heard or seen the likes", said Ann.

In our completion circle, I said, "The gift I

take with me today is my willingness to believe the unbelievable; to truly live and dwell in the realm of Possibility. I've experienced a day of Mystery and Miracles. Thank you All! Thank you, Rama!"

Further Examination and Process

Ask yourself, what is it horse wants of me? In my heart, I know……..? What might be the equine perspective?

Somewhere in the mix (of the NARHA-EFMHA merger) is the necessity of including potential horse professionals and instructors in an EFL session. Once one has personally experienced work in the Field Awareness of Horse learning from Heart of Horse, one is changed, different, and sees with other than the five ordinary senses of the concretized world; the world is experienced from a fresh perspective.

The AIA heart lens process connects mind, body and heart in relationship with a sentient being, the horse. AIA engages the Sacred while exercising the body, calming the mind, and nurturing the Soul. Working with and Riding horses may be experienced as "Joyful meditation in motion". It is a significant opportunity to expand cross-species communication while enjoying the healing ambiance of Nature.

EPILOGUE

MEMOIR BOOK ON CAPACITIES

Mom's ghost segues into Rama's Magic where we begin to discuss and discern insights of practice-recall earlier introduction of Rama -"A word about our personal horses."

The other morning I slowly awakened feeling fresh. Vitalized and aware I was surfacing from a Power Dream of children's father Ram plotting/studying how to return to MorningStar and "rescue" Mom, his first Mother-in-law. He had always "blamed" Mom's influence on me and the kids with distrust and alarm.

More to come with Rama's continued work at TROT, AIA, Al-Marah and Prescott's Chapel

Rock and Horses of Hope in Baxter Springs, Kansas, Lucky Pup Ranch in Bisbee, Arizona, Apache Spring's Ranch in Sonoita, Veterans story, Happy-ever-After Horse.

Book two deals with the federal agents and Rama's work with them. Doctor Larry Shamus, DVM, and Rama as the Happy-Ever-After Horse. I will share Holly's story and Wyatt and the Harley Ride. We will also cover Brian and his tutoring as our rental tenant in Flagstaff.

ACKNOWLEDGMENTS

Thanks to:

Pat McNees, Editor

Sam and PJ Turner, Editors

Sweet 'N Spicy Designs, Formatting and Cover Design